HAVING
OUR SAY

G·K
Hall
&C⁰·

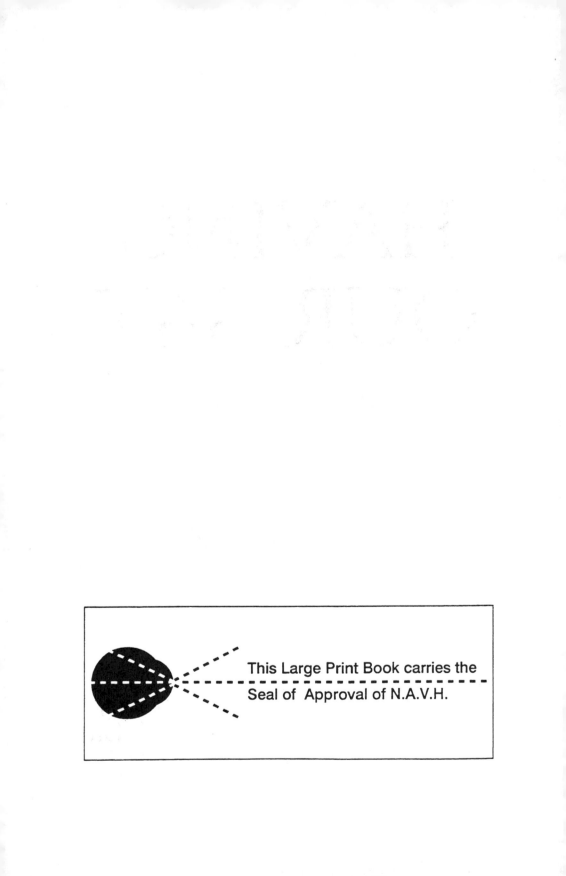

HAVING OUR SAY

The Delany Sisters'
First 100 Years

Sarah and A. Elizabeth Delany
with Amy Hill Hearth

G.K. Hall & Co.
Thorndike, Maine

The contemporary photographs of Sadie and Bessie Delany
were taken by Brian Douglas. All other photographs are from
the authors' collection.

Published in Large Print by arrangement with Kodansha
America, Inc.

G.K. Hall Large Print Book Series.

Set in 16 pt. News Plantin by Melissa Harvey.

Printed on acid free paper in the United States of America.

Library of Congress Cataloging-in-Publication Data

Delany, Sarah Louise, 1889–
    Having our say : the Delany sisters' first 100 years /
Sarah and A. Elizabeth Delany, with Amy Hill Hearth.
        p. cm.
    ISBN 0-8161-5830-4 (alk. paper : lg. print)
    ISBN 0-8161-5831-2 (alk. paper : lg. print : pbk)
    1. Afro-Americans—Biography. 2. Delany family.
3. Delany, Sarah Louise, 1889– . 4. Delany, Annie Elizabeth,
1891– . 5. United Sates—Race relations. 6. Large type books.
I. Delany, Annie Elizabeth, 1891– . II. Hearth, Amy Hill, 1958– .
III. Title.
[E185.96.D37   1993b]
973'.0496073'00922—dc20
    [B]   93-24264
                                                              CIP

DEDICATED TO

HENRY BEARD DELANY (1858–1928)
and NANNY LOGAN DELANY (1861–1956)
and to
BLAIR A. T. HEARTH

The authors would like to thank Elisa Petrini, Milton R. Bass, Harry Henderson, and Dr. James A. Boyer for their assistance and support in creating this book.

Contents

FAMILY TREE

DELANY FAMILY
St. Marys, Georgia

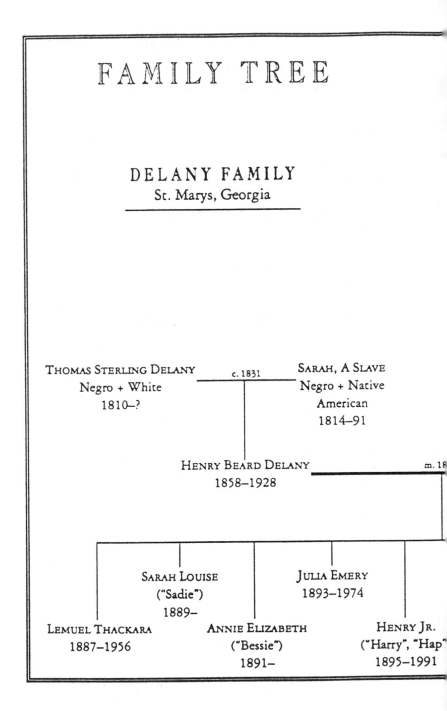

THOMAS STERLING DELANY
Negro + White
1810–?

c. 1831

SARAH, A SLAVE
Negro + Native
American
1814–91

HENRY BEARD DELANY
1858–1928

m. 18

LEMUEL THACKARA
1887–1956

SARAH LOUISE
("Sadie")
1889–

ANNIE ELIZABETH
("Bessie")
1891–

JULIA EMERY
1893–1974

HENRY JR.
("Harry", "Hap"
1895–1991

LOGAN FAMILY
Danville, Virginia Area

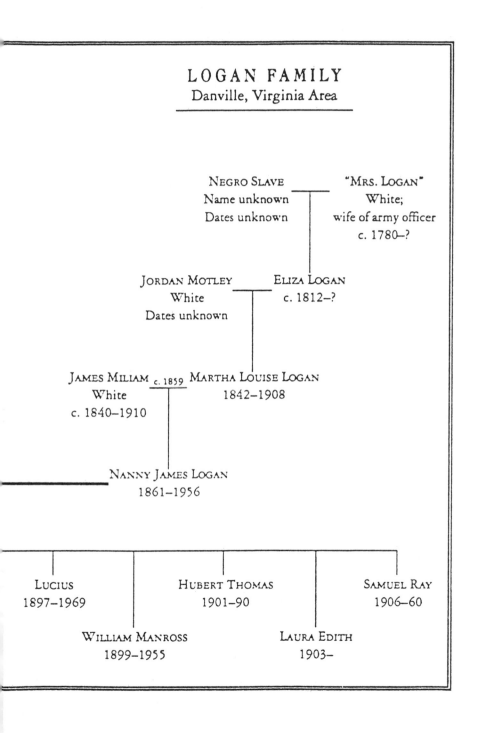

NEGRO SLAVE
Name unknown
Dates unknown

"MRS. LOGAN"
White;
wife of army officer
c. 1780–?

JORDAN MOTLEY
White
Dates unknown

ELIZA LOGAN
c. 1812–?

JAMES MILIAM
White
c. 1840–1910

c. 1859

MARTHA LOUISE LOGAN
1842–1908

NANNY JAMES LOGAN
1861–1956

LUCIUS
1897–1969

HUBERT THOMAS
1901–90

SAMUEL RAY
1906–60

WILLIAM MANROSS
1899–1955

LAURA EDITH
1903–

PREFACE

When I met Sadie Delany and her sister, Bessie, in September 1991, I was on assignment for *The New York Times*, hoping to write a story on these two elderly but reclusive sisters who had just celebrated their one-hundred-and-second and one-hundredth birthdays. In my hand I carried a letter written by their neighbor in Mount Vernon, New York, who had extended an invitation to come by and meet them. The Delany sisters had no phone, so I wasn't entirely sure they knew I was coming. I was prepared to be turned away.

I knocked on the door. I waited and raised my hand to knock again, when suddenly the door swung open. The woman who answered, with her head held high, her eyes intense and penetrating, extended her hand in formal greeting. "I am Dr. Delany," she said elegantly.

She ushered me into the house, and from across the room, another elderly woman said sweetly, "Please come in, child. Won't you sit down?" This was the elder sister, Sadie Delany.

I must have hesitated for a moment. "Go on, sit down," Bessie urged. "Sit down as long as you like. We won't charge you rent!" Then they both laughed uproariously at this little joke.

Over the next three hours, I was charmed by their vivaciousness and playfulness. They seemed to have conquered old age, or to have come as close to it as anyone ever will. It was clear that they had found the source of their vitality in each other's company, and in the tales they told and retold each other from a century of living.

When my piece was published, the reaction was swift. Readers fell in love with the Delany sisters. There were letters from all over the country, demands for television interviews, requests for guest appearances at schools and at political functions. The sisters declined nearly all of the invitations.

Among those who read my article were editors at Kodansha America, Inc., who felt that the Delanys' story deserved to be a book. At first the sisters demurred, unsure that their life stories were sufficiently interesting or significant. But they came to see that by recording their story, they were participating in a tradition as old as time: the passing of knowledge and experience from one generation to the next.

The daughters of a man born into slavery and a mother of mixed racial parentage who was born free, the sisters recall what it meant to be "colored" children in the late nineteenth century in the South. Their early lives were sheltered: They grew up on a college campus, Saint Augustine's School in Raleigh, North Carolina, where their father was an Episcopal priest and vice principal. Despite their privileged status, they suffered the insult of Jim Crow when it first became law.

After years of teaching in the rural South to raise money, the Delany sisters joined the great wave of black Americans who headed north in search of opportunity during the early part of this century. Bessie became only the second black woman licensed to practice dentistry in New York, and Sadie was the first black person ever to teach domestic science on the high school level in New York City public schools.

The sisters lived in Harlem, and were acquainted with such legendary figures as the statesman and poet James Weldon Johnson and the entertainer Cab Calloway. During an era when hearth and home defined the place of women, the Delany sisters spurned marriage opportunities for careers. In the 1950s they were in the vanguard of middle-class black Americans who integrated the suburbs and faced a new and difficult set of challenges. Already elderly in the 1960s, they cheered from the sidelines as the civil rights movement flourished, praying and worrying about younger relatives who were getting caught up in the protests.

Each sister developed her own way of coping within a racist society. Sadie expertly "played dumb" and manipulated the system, and Bessie believed in confrontation, regardless of the cost. This difference in personal styles has brought balance — and occasionally fireworks — to their hun-

13

dred-year companionship. "We are living proof that you don't change one bit from cradle to grave," Bessie likes to say.

This book is woven from thousands of anecdotes that I coaxed from the Delany sisters during an eighteen-month period (September 1991 to April 1993). The sequence of stories is mine but the words are all theirs. At times the sisters' versions of particular events were almost identical or told in a joint fashion — with one sister beginning a sentence, and the other finishing it — and so some chapters bear both of their names. In the others, either Sadie or Bessie chronicles their life together, each with her own distinct spin, voice, and viewpoint. Their story, as the Delany sisters like to say, is not meant as "black" or "women's" history, but American history. It belongs to all of us.

One final note: During the past year, many people have attempted to locate the Delany sisters. The Delany sisters regret that they cannot entertain visitors. To protect their health and privacy, the sisters have requested that correspondence be limited to letters only, and sent in care of Kodansha America, Inc., 114 Fifth Avenue, New York, New York 10011.

AMY HILL HEARTH
Westchester County, New York
April 2, 1993

PART I

SWEET SADIE, QUEEN BESS

Both more than one hundred years old, Sarah ("Sadie") Delany and her sister, Annie Elizabeth ("Bessie") Delany are among the oldest living witnesses to American history. They are also the oldest surviving members of one of the nation's preeminent black families, which rose to prominence just one generation after the Civil War.

Few families have ever achieved so much so quickly. Henry Beard Delany, the sisters' father, was born into slavery but eventually became the first elected "Negro" bishop of the Episcopal Church, U.S.A. All ten of his children were college-educated professionals at a time when few Americans — black or white — ever went beyond high school.

In the white world, with the possible exception of Hubert, the sisters' younger brother who was a New York political leader, the Delanys were almost unknown. But in the black society of Raleigh, North Carolina, where they grew up, and later in Harlem, the Delanys were legendary. Gail

Lumet Buckley, daughter of the actress and singer Lena Horne, ranks the Delanys among the black intelligentsia in her family memoir, *The Hornes*: "The Hornes were by no means peerless. . . . More noteworthy in terms of ACHIEVEMENT were, to name just a few, the Hunts and Bonds of Georgia, the Langstons of Ohio, the Delanys of North Carolina, and the Robesons of New Jersey. . . ."

The black press chronicled their remarkable achievements and held them up as role models. "The Delanys present a unique picture of family success," declared New York's *Amsterdam News* in 1951. "The saga of the Delany family emerges as a symbol of the Negro's struggle for survival, achievement and service," trumpeted *The People's Voice* in an editorial published in September 1942. And an article in *Ebony* magazine titled "Negro Blue Bloods" cited the Delanys' accomplishments, quoting their mother, Nanny Logan Delany, as saying, "It's no more than they should have done."

The Delanys had to face some surprising detractors. Sadie and Bessie recall that lower-class blacks at times viewed achievers as being cliquish or arrogant, and that some cautioned that families such as the Delanys set impossibly high standards for other black Americans of that era. Their success, some felt, set up the larger black community for criticism by white America: If they can do it, why can't the rest of you?

The Delany creed centered on self-improvement through education, civic-mindedness, and ethical living, along with a strong belief in God. The family motto was, "Your job is to help somebody." According to Bessie and Sadie Delany, this code applied to anyone who needed help, regardless of color. Their accomplishments could not shield them from discrimination and the pain of racism, but they held themselves to high standards of fair-minded idealism.

Today the Delanys are no longer concentrated in Raleigh or Harlem. As in most American families, the younger generation — among them teachers, entrepreneurs, physicians, attorneys, and other professionals — is scattered from coast to coast. At least once a year, however, everyone seems to find the time to journey to Mount Vernon, New York, to see the family matriarchs, Aunt Sadie and Aunt Bessie, the custodians of the Delany legacy.

1

SADIE

Bessie and I have been together since time began, or so it seems. Bessie is my little sister, only she's not so little.

She is 101 years old, and I am 103.

People always say they'd like to live to be one hundred, but no one really expects to, except Bessie. She always said she planned to be as old as Moses. And when Bessie says she's going to do something, she does it. Now, I think Moses lived to 120. So I told Bessie that if she lives to 120, then I'll just have to live to 122 so I can take care of her.

Neither one of us ever married and we've lived together most all of our lives, and probably know each other better than any two human beings on this Earth. After so long, we are in some ways like one person. She is my right arm. If she were to die first, I'm not sure if I would want to go on living because the reason I am living is to keep *her* living.

Bessie and I still keep house by ourselves. We

still do our shopping and banking. We were in helping professions — Bessie was a dentist and I was a high school teacher — so we're not rich, but we get by. Papa always taught us that with every dollar you earn, the first ten cents goes to the Lord, the second goes in the bank for hard times, and the rest is yours, but you better spend it wisely. Well, it's a good thing we listened because we're living on that hard-time money now, and not doing too badly.

We've buried so many people we've loved; that is the hard part of living this long. Most everyone we know has turned to dust. Well, there must be some reason we're still here. That's why we agreed to do this book; it gives us a sense of purpose. If it helps just one person, then it's worth doing. That's what Mama used to say.

Bessie and I have lived in New York for the last seventy-five years, but Raleigh will always be home. Raleigh is where Mama and Papa met, as students at Saint Augustine's School, which was a school for Negroes. Mama and Papa got married in the campus chapel back in 1886 and raised all ten of us children right there at good old "Saint Aug's." Papa became vice principal and Mama was the matron, which meant she ran things day-to-day at the school.

I don't remember my mother ever calling my father by his first name, Henry. He was always "Mr. Delany" or "Your Pa." Now, I do recall that my father would call my mother "Miss Nan" in private moments, but he usually called her Mrs.

21

Delany in front of everyone, including us children. Now, you might think this seems a bit formal. But the reason they did this is that colored people were always called by their first names in that era. It was a way of treating them with less dignity. What Mama and Papa were doing was blocking that. Most people never learned their first names.

In 1918 Papa became the first elected Negro bishop of the Episcopal Church, U.S.A. That's a long way for a man who was born a slave on a Georgia plantation. But if you had known Papa, you wouldn't be surprised. He was always improving himself, and he and Mama brought us up to reach high.

Papa was a smart, good-looking Negro man. Actually, his skin was a reddish-brown, on account of his mother being part Indian. Mama, who was from Virginia, was an issue-free Negro.* Mama looked white but she never did try to "pass." She was proud to be a colored woman!

People would look at us Delany children and wonder where in the world this bunch came from. We were every different shade from nearly white to brown-sugar. I was one of the lighter children, and Bessie was browner. As children, we were aware we were colored but we never gave it a second thought. Papa was dark and Mama was light and so what? It's just the way it was.

I came into this world at 7:30 in the evening on the nineteenth day of September, 1889. It was a

---

*An issue-free Negro was a person who had some black ancestry but whose mother was a free person, not a slave.

long day of hard labor for Mama. Poor, dear Papa! There wasn't a thing he could do for Mama but worry and pray.

Everyone was nervous, because I was Mama's second baby, and the doctor had to be brought in after my older brother, Lemuel, was born two years earlier. This time, Mama wanted her sister, Eliza, by her side. That's why I was born at Lynch's Station, Virginia, where Eliza lived. Mama just got on that old train and headed up there when she was about ready to drop me.

Eliza's presence was calming, and the doctor was not needed. As a matter of fact, after the midwife left, Mama sat up in bed and declared she was hungry! Eliza was just tickled to death at Mama's appetite and cooked up the biggest plate of fried apples and hot biscuits Mama ever saw. Mama said she ate every bite. They named me Sarah Louise, but I have always been called Sadie.

Mama got her confidence back with my birth, and went on to have eight more healthy babies. Next in line was Annie Elizabeth, born two years after me and known as Bessie. I don't remember life without Bessie.

"Queen Bess," as Papa used to call her, was born on the third of September, 1891. Like all my younger brothers and sisters, she was born in Raleigh. She arrived at 9:30 in the morning, after keeping poor Mama up all night pacing those pine floorboards, which creaked loud enough to wake the dead. Bessie was so alert at birth that Mama said she had a funny feeling that child

23

would have a mind of her own.

Bessie was what we used to call a "feeling" child; she was sensitive and emotional. She was quick to anger, and very outspoken. Now, I was a "mama's child" and followed my Mama around like a shadow. I always did what I was told. I was calm and agreeable. The way I see it, there's room in the world for both me and Bessie. We kind of balance each other out.

2

BESSIE

People learned not to mess with me from Day One. When I was small, a neighborhood girl started taunting me: "Bessie Delany, you scrawny thing. You've got the skinniest legs and the longest neck I ever did see." Now, this girl was a bully, and I had seen her technique before: She would say nasty things to other girls, and they'd burst into tears and run crying to their mama. She was a lot bigger than me, but I didn't care. I said, "Oh, why don't you shut up. You ain't so pretty yourself!" And she never bothered me again.

Papa used to say, "You catch more flies with molasses than vinegar." He believed you could get further in life by being nice to people. Well, this is easy for Sadie to swallow. Sadie is molasses without even trying! She can sweet-talk the world, or play dumb, or whatever it takes to get by without a fuss. But even as a tiny little child, I wasn't afraid of anything. I'd meet the Devil before day and look him in the eye, no matter what the price. If Sadie is molasses, then I am vinegar! Sadie is sugar, and I'm the spice.

You know, Sadie doesn't approve of me sometimes. She frowns at me in her big-sister-sort-of-way and says it's a wonder I wasn't lynched. Well, it's true I almost was. But I'm still here, yes, sir!

What worries me is that I know Sadie's going to get into Heaven, but I'm not so sure about me. I'm working on it, but it sure is hard to change. I've been trying to change for one hundred years without success, that's not so good, is it? I'm afraid when I meet St. Peter at the Gate, he'll say, "Lord, child, you were *mean!*"

I have trouble with the idea of forgiving and forgetting. You see, I can forgive, but I can't seem to forget. And I'm not sure the Lord would approve of that at all. I remember things that happened long, long ago that still make me madder than a hornet. I wish they didn't. Most of the things that make me mad happened to me because I am colored. As a woman dentist, I faced sexual harassment — that's what they call it today — but to me, racism was always a bigger problem.

Most of the people I'm still mad at are long dead. If I say something mean about them, Sadie will say, "Now Bessie, of the dead say nothing Evil." And I try to be good.

Sometimes I am angry at all white people, until I stop and think of the nice white people I have known in my life. OK, OK, there have been a few. I admit it. And my mother is part white, and I can't hate my own flesh and blood! There are good white people out there. Sometimes, they

26

are hard to find, but they're out there, just look for them.

But the rebby boys tend to stand out, make themselves known. Rebby is what we used to call racist white men. I guess it's short for rebel. I'll tell you, the way those rebby types treat colored folks — well, it just makes me sick. If I had a pet buzzard I'd treat him better than the way some white folks have treated me! There isn't a Negro this side of Glory who doesn't know exactly what I mean.

Why, the rebby boys start early in life learning to hate. I remember encountering some who weren't more than ten or twelve years old. They were cutting through the fields at Saint Aug's one day, and I had strayed a few yards from where I was supposed to be. I was about six years old. My little petticoat had slipped down a bit, and they made some nasty remarks about this little colored girl and her underpants. I'm not even sure I understood what they were saying, but I got their meaning.

The rebby boys don't give colored folks credit for a thing, not a single thing. Why, I think we've done pretty well, considering we were dragged over here in chains from Africa! Why, colored folks *built* this country, and that is the truth. We were the laborers, honey! And even after we were freed, we were the backbone of this country — the maids, cooks, undertakers, barbers, porters, and so on.

Those rebby types! What do they think, anyway? When we get to the Spirit World, do they think colored people are going to be waiting on their tables, pouring their tea? I think some of them are in for a big surprise. They're going to be pouring tea for *me*.

Now, Sadie doesn't get all agitated like this. She just shrugs it off. It's been a little harder for me, partly because I'm darker than she is, and the darker you are, honey, the harder it is. But it's also been harder on me because I have a different personality than Sadie. She is a true Christian woman! I wish I were more like her but I'm afraid I am a naughty little darkey! Ha ha! I know it's not fashionable to use some of the words from my heyday, but that's who I am! And who is going to stop me? Nobody, that's who! Ain't nobody going to censor *me*, no, sir! I'm a hundred-and-one years old and at my age, honey, I can say what I want!

Now, don't go thinking that I'm *all* mean. I am not so angry that I cannot laugh at myself! One thing most Negroes learn early is how to laugh at their situation.

If you asked me the secret to longevity, I would tell you that you have to work at taking care of your health. But a lot of it's attitude. I'm alive out of sheer determination, honey! Sometimes I think it's my *meanness* that keeps me going.

3

SADIE

Every morning, I ask Bessie: "Are we going to have any visitors today?" And she will stop and get real quiet and think real hard and say, "No, we are not." Or she'll say, "Yes, so-and-so will be coming." And generally she is right.

You see, Bessie believes she is a little psychic. I try not to encourage this, because it's ungodly. But I have to admit, Bessie is a little, well, *intuitive.*

Years ago, Mama tried to discourage Bessie from indulging her psychic abilities. Bessie wanted to go to a palm reader but Mama wouldn't let her. Mama frowned on the whole matter. It just wasn't something that nice Christian girls were supposed to do.

But over the years, I've come to think that Bessie really does have some special talents. And I admit that it often comes in handy. You see, we don't have a telephone. We have to rely on the U.S. mail and on Bessie's intuition.

Everybody is always after us to get a phone.

We hate phones! Of course, we had a phone years ago when Bessie was a practicing dentist. We had to, and that was OK. But ever since we moved to this house, in 1957, we have not had a phone. If we have an emergency, we have a light we put on in the house that we never use otherwise, and somebody always comes running over here right away.

The phone company came by and pestered us. Finally we told the man, "Mister, if the phone company installed a phone for free and paid for a man to stand there and answer it for us, seven days a week, we *still* wouldn't want a phone!" He got the message.

The world is a puzzling place today. All these banks sending us credit cards, with our names on them. Well, we didn't order any credit cards! We don't spend what we don't have. So we just cut them in half and throw them out, just as soon as we open them in the mail. Imagine a bank sending credit cards to two ladies over a hundred years old! What are those folks thinking?

One time, I got this nasty letter from the New York City Board of Education. They wanted to cut off my pension. They demanded that I prove I am still alive! I guess they thought I was long dead and somebody was stealing my check. Well, we got it all straightened out, but you know that is the type of thing you have to deal with, when you get to be our age.

Sometimes we get pestered by people who just show up at the door. You never know who it's going to be. The most persistent are these folks who go door-to-door, evangelizing. I just look at them through the window, and shake my head no. I won't even open the door. But sometimes Bessie will go upstairs and open the window, stick her head out, and call down to them. She'll say:

"What do you want?"

And they'll say, "We just want to talk to you for a minute."

And Bessie'll say, "Oh, no, you don't! You don't want to talk! You want to *convert* me. And I'm more than a hundred years old, and I've been an Episcopalian all my life, and ain't nobody going to derail me or my sister now!" Bessie always has to get into a fuss. We really don't have time for this kind of mischief. We have a lot to do — bills to pay, letters to write, food to prepare! People don't understand this. They think we're sitting around in rocking chairs, which isn't at all true. Why, we don't even own a rocking chair.

I'll tell you something about Bessie. She has made a full-time job out of watching over the whole neighborhood. She's always looking out the window and reporting to me what so-and-so is doing. I say, "Now, Bessie, is that really your business?" And she says, "If it's going on in my neighborhood, it's my business." And I say, "Bessie, you are a nosy old gal." And she says, "Sister Sadie, we bought a house with windows, those windows are here for a reason, and I'm going to use them!"

Sometimes, she gets really mad at me and says,

"You wouldn't care if the whole neighborhood was burning down around us!" Of course, that's not true, and she knows it. She just gets mad 'cause I'm not as nosy as she is.

4

BESSIE

I'll tell you a story: The house we own is a two-family house, and sometimes the neighbors can hear us through the wall. One time, they had a guest who was up in arms. Just up in arms! She heard these sounds, like laughter, coming from our side, late at night, and she was convinced there were ha'ants. Yes, sir, she thought we were ghosts.

Our neighbor came over the next day and quizzed us down. And I said, "Ain't no ha'ants, it's just the two of us being silly." It hadn't occurred to them that these two old sisters, at our age, would be a-carrying on like that. I guess they think of old folks as people who sit around like old sourpusses. But not us. No, sir! When people ask me how we've lived past one hundred, I say, "Honey, we never married. We never had husbands to worry us to death!"

I love to laugh. There's a song I just remembered from the 1890s that we colored children used to sing. Sadie and I thought it was hilarious. I hadn't thought of it in, well, about a hundred years! It goes like this:

The preacher he went a-hunting
On one Sunday morn
According to his religion
He carried along his gun
He shot one dozen partridges
On his way to the fair
And he got down the road a little further
And spied a big, grizzly bear
Well, the bear stood up in the middle
  of the road
The coon dropped to his knees
He was so excited
That he climbed up in a tree!
The parson stayed in that tree
I think it was all night
Then he cast his eyes to the Lord in
  the sky
And these words said to him
Oh Lord, didn't you deliver Daniel
From the lion's den?
Also brother Jonah
From the belly of the whale,
And when the three Hebrew children
In the fiery furnace sent?
Oh Lord, please me do spare!
But Lord, if you can't help me,
Please don't help that bear!

Honey, we thought that punch line at the end

was just about the funniest thing in the world. Oppressed people have a good sense of humor. Think of the Jews. They know how to laugh, and to laugh at themselves! Well, we colored folks are the same way. We colored folks are survivors.

There are certain stereotypes that are offensive. Some of them don't worry me, though. For instance, I have always thought that Mammy character in *Gone with the Wind* was mighty funny. And I just loved "Amos 'n' Andy" on the radio. So you see, I have enough confidence in myself that those things did not bother me. I could laugh.

Sadie and I get a kick out of things that happened a long, long time ago. We talk about folks who turned to dust so long ago that we're the only people left on this Earth with any memory of them. We always find ways to celebrate our memories of our family and friends. Why, we still have a birthday party for Papa, even though he's been gone since 1928. We cook his favorite birthday meal, just the way he liked it: chicken and gravy, rice and sweet potatoes, ham, macaroni and cheese, cabbage, cauliflower, broccoli, turnips, and carrots. For dessert we'll have a birthday cake — a pound cake — and ambrosia, made with oranges and fresh coconut.

Generally, we stay away from liquor. Except once in a while, we make Jell-o with wine. What you do is replace some of the water in the recipe with wine. It'll relax you, but you won't get drunk. The truth is, I have never been *drunk* in my life.

One thing Sadie and I do is stay away from doctors as much as possible. And we avoid hospitals because, honey, they'll kill you there. They overtreat you. And when they see how old you are, and that you still have a mind, they treat you like a curiosity: like "Exhibit A" and "Exhibit B." Like, "Hey, nurse, come on over here and looky-here at this old woman, she's in such good shape. . . ." Most of the time they don't even treat you like a person, just an object.

One time, some doctor asked Sadie to do a senility test. Of course, she passed. A year later, he asked her to do it again, and she said, "Don't waste your time, doctor." And she answered all the questions from the year before, before he could ask them. And then she said to me, "Come on, Bess, let's get on out of here."

People assume Sadie and I don't have any sense at our age. But we still have all our marbles, yes, sir! I do get tired, physically. But how can I complain about being tired? God don't ever get tired of putting his sun out every morning, does He? Who am I to complain about being weary?

Funny thing is, some days I feel like a young girl and other days I'm feeling the grave, just a-feeling the grave. That's why it's important that we get all this stuff written down now, because you never know when you'll meet the Lord in the sky.

PART II

"I AM FREE!"

SADIE and Bessie's father, Henry Beard Delany, was born into slavery and came of age at a time of tremendous upheaval in the South. When the bloody Civil War came to a close, the South was left in ruins. The decade of Reconstruction that followed was an unstable and violent era, marked by power struggles between the North and South about how the postwar transition should proceed. Caught in the middle were four million freed slaves, who mostly lived in conditions not much improved from captivity.

The Delanys fared better than most. Because they had been "house niggers," the Delanys had been forced to endure comparatively fewer privations than those who labored in the fields. Most important, they could read and write, and were better able than many former slaves to make a niche for themselves in the chaos of Southern life.

The Delany sisters' maternal ancestors, the Logans of Virginia, held an even more ambiguous place in the social order. They were free Negroes —

not enslaved yet not accepted as citizens before the Civil War. In 1860 there were perhaps 250,000 free Negroes in the slaveholding states, mostly former slaves who had been freed. Their numbers were swollen by laws mandating that people of mixed race be classified as "colored," even if they appeared white. Accounts of the lives of these free-men and -women in the South are not widely known, and the Logan family story illustrates some of the problems they faced.

By the time that Henry Delany and Nanny Logan married in 1886, a black middle class had begun to evolve in the South. Similar to the black leadership class in the North, which had an earlier start, the success of the Southern middle class was based on entrepreneurship. Most of the new black-owned businesses were aimed at black consumers, for in many places, interracial trading was prohibited by custom or by law. The Delanys recall, for example, that some family friends who were black had built a successful undertaking business which at first served whites as well as blacks. That business nearly collapsed, however, when a law was passed in North Carolina that made it illegal for black undertakers to serve the white community.

Regardless of achievement or economic status, no black person could hope to escape the stigma of color. The Civil War had ended in 1865, but white America was not ready to surrender its belief in Negro inferiority, the rationale that had helped create the institution of slavery.

5

SADIE AND BESSIE

Our Papa's People

On February 5, 1858, our Papa, Henry Beard Delany, was born into slavery on a plantation owned by the Mock family in St. Marys, Georgia, on the coast near the Florida border. He was just a little bitty fellow — seven years old — when the Surrender came in 1865. "The Surrender" is the way Papa always referred to the end of the Civil War, when General Robert E. Lee surrendered to the Union at Appomattox Court House.

We used to ask Papa, "What do you remember about being a slave?" Well, like a lot of former slaves he didn't say much about it. Everybody had their own tale of woe and for most people, things had been so bad they didn't want to think about it, let alone talk about it. You didn't sit and cry in your soup, honey, you just went on.

Well, we persisted, and finally Papa told us of the day his people were freed. He remembered being in the kitchen and wearing a little apron, which little slave boys wore in those days. It had one button at the top, at the back of the neck,

41

and the ends were loose. And when the news of the Surrender came, he said he ran about the house with that apron fluttering behind him, yelling, "Freedom! Freedom! I am free! I am free!"

Of course, being a little child, he did not know what this meant. Back in slavery days, things were bad, but in some ways getting your freedom could be worse! To a small boy, it meant leaving the only home you ever knew.

Now, Papa's family were house niggers, and the Mocks had been very good to them. We remember our Papa saying the Mocks were as good as any people you could find anywhere in this world. That's a generous thing to say about the people who *owned* him, wouldn't you say? But he said that not all white people who owned slaves were evil. There was great variety in the way white people treated Negroes. That's what Papa told us about slavery days, and it's true now, too.

Mrs. Mock thought a heap of Papa's mother, Sarah, who was born on the plantation on the fifth of January, 1814. Why, Mrs. Mock had even let Sarah have a wedding ceremony in the front parlor. It was a double wedding — Sarah's twin sister, Mary, married at the same time. Oh, it was said to be a big affair! Of course, these weren't legal marriages, since it was against the law for slaves to get married. But it was a ceremony, and Sarah was joined in matrimony to Thomas Sterling Delany. This was about 1831. Their first child, Julia, was born on the first of November, 1832. Altogether, Sarah and Thomas had eleven chil-

42

dren, and our Papa was the youngest.

Thomas was a handsome man. To what extent he was white, we do not know. We were told he was mostly Negro. The family Bible says he was born in St. Marys, and the date of his birth was the fifteenth of March, 1810.

Sarah was obviously part Indian; she had long, straight black hair but otherwise looked just like a Negro. When we were children we always giggled about her photograph, because her hair looked so peculiar to us. We never knew Papa's parents because they died when we were tiny. Why, Sarah died on the eleventh of September, 1891, just a few days after Bessie was born.

Thomas was part Scottish, which is where the Delany name came from. We have been asked, over the years, if we are any kin to Martin Delany, the Negro army officer during the Civil War. We are quite certain we are not, having discussed it with a historian once. People assume that we are related to him because we spell Delany the same way. A few of our relatives spell our name with an "e", as in "Delaney," which is really an Irish spelling. Others spell it "DeLany" with a capital L in the middle. Papa insisted we spell it "Delany." He said, "That's the way my father spelled it, and that's good enough for me."

Now, of course, we haven't any idea what our original African name was. But it doesn't worry us none. We have been Delanys for a long time, and the name belongs to us, as far as we're concerned.

The Mocks let the Delanys keep their name and even broke Georgia law by teaching Papa and his brothers and sisters to read and write. Maybe the Mocks thought the Delanys wouldn't leave, after the Surrender. But they did, and they each didn't have but the shirt on their backs. They crossed the St. Marys River and set down roots in Fernandina Beach, Florida. Papa told us that each day they would wash their only shirt in the river and hang it up to dry, then put it on again after it had dried in the sun.

Those were hard times, after slavery days. Much of the South was scarred by the Civil War and there wasn't much food or supplies among the whites, let alone the Negroes. Most of the slaves, when they were freed, wandered about the countryside like shell-shocked soldiers. Papa said everywhere you went, it seemed you saw Negroes asking, begging for something. He said it was a pitiful sight.

He said those folks didn't know how to be free. It was like if you took the hen away, what do you think would happen to those chicks?

Most of the slaves became sharecroppers, living off the land owned by whites. The whites fixed it so those Negroes could never get ahead. Wasn't much better than slavery. The whites were able to cheat the Negroes because very few Negroes could read or write or do arithmetic. And even if the Negroes knew they were being cheated, there wasn't a thing they could do about it.

The Delanys were among only a handful of former slaves in those parts who didn't end up begging. Papa was proud of this, beyond words. They survived by eating fish they caught in the river and gathering up wild plants for food. After a while, they built a home, some kind of lean-to or log cabin. They were smart, but they were lucky, and they knew it. They could read and write, and they hadn't been abused, and their family was still together. That's a lot more than most former slaves had going for them.

Papa and his brothers all learned a trade. Following in the shoes of one of his older brothers, Papa became a mason. His brother was known in the South for being able to figure the number of bricks it would take to build a house. People would send him drawings and that fellow could figure out in his head exactly how many bricks it would take! Saved people a lot of trouble and money. Another of Papa's brothers was said to be the first Negro harbor pilot in America, and his older sister, Mary, taught school, mostly at night to poor colored men who worked all day in the field.

The Delanys were Methodists through and through. Papa was already a grown man, in his early twenties, when one day the Reverend Owen Thackara, a white Episcopal priest, said to him, "Young man, you should go to college." The chance to go to college was so fantastic it boggled Papa's mind, and of course he jumped at the chance, even though it meant giving up on being a Methodist. Reverend Thackara helped Papa go to Saint Augustine's School, way north in Raleigh, in the great state of North Carolina.

Well, Papa did not disappoint anyone. In college, he was a shining star among shining stars. He was as smart as he could be, and blessed with a personality that smoothed the waters. He soon met a fellow student named Nanny James Logan, the belle of the campus. She was a pretty gal and very popular, despite the fact that she was smarter than all the boys — and became the class valedictorian.

6

SADIE AND BESSIE

Our Mama's People

Miss Logan, who would one day be our Mama, was born in Virginia in a community called Yak, seven miles outside Danville. Today, they call it Mountain Hill. Guess they think that sounds better than Yak.

Miss Nanny Logan was a feisty thing, a trait which she could have gotten from either of her parents. Her father, James Miliam, was 100 percent white, and the meanest-looking man in Pittsylvania County, Virginia. Because he was white, he could not legally marry his ladylove, Nanny's mother, an issue-free Negro named Martha Logan.

This is what we were told by our Mama: A fellow named John Logan, who was white, was an army officer called away to fight during the War of 1812. While he was gone, his wife took up with a Negro slave on their plantation. She was already the mother of seven daughters by her husband, and her romance with the slave produced two more daughters. When the husband returned, he forgave his wife — *forgave her!* — and adopted the two mulatto girls as his own. They even took his last name, Logan. No one remembers what happened to the slave, except he must've left town in a big hurry. This slave and this white woman were our great-great-grandparents.

The two little mulatto girls, Patricia and Eliza, were just part of the family. The only time anyone has heard tell of their older, white half sisters mistreating them was when those white girls were old enough to start courting and they used to hide their little, colored half sisters! One time, they hid them in a hogshead barrel and after their gentlemen callers left, they couldn't get them out! Patricia was entirely stuck, and they had to use an ax on that old barrel to get her out. Well, they slipped and cut Patricia's leg, and she carried that scar on her knee to the grave.

When Patricia grew up, she had ten children. One thing we remember about her was that one of her babies was born on the side of the road. She would walk to the mill to get her corn ground, carrying this big sack on her head. On the way back one day, she went into labor and could not get home in time. So she had that baby on the side of the road, by herself! And afterward, she just put that baby under her arm, and that sack of cornmeal back on her head, and walked on home.

Patricia's sister, Eliza, meantime, had become involved with a white man named Jordan Motley. They had a child — Martha Louise Logan, our grandma, born in 1842. Eliza had three other daughters: Blanche, LaTisha, and Narcissa, who was the prettiest one of the four girls but never married. Whether those three girls all had the same Pa, we do not know.

They were charmers, all four of those girls, and very popular, but it's said they squabbled quite a bit. Why, our Mama remembered as a little child throwing salt in the fire to put out their fussing. People in those days thought that would stop an argument. Well, Mama said she must've thrown a peck of salt in the fire, trying to put out the fussing between her mother and her mother's three sisters!

One thing's for sure: Those four girls were all only one-quarter Negro, but in the eyes of the world they were colored. It only took one drop of Negro blood for a person to be considered "colored." So Martha Logan and her sisters were in a bind when it came to marrying. If they wanted to marry a colored man, well, most of them were slaves. And they couldn't marry white, because it was illegal for Negroes and whites to marry in Virginia at that time, and for many years after — until 1967! Well, it didn't stop them from having love relationships. Martha Logan took up with a man named James Miliam, who was as white as he could be. We remember our grandparents well because we used to go visit every summer, and we were young women when they died.

One time, James and Grandma had a big fuss, and to this day we don't know what it was about.

We think it had to do with race, that he made some remark about little nigger children or the like, because all of a sudden Grandma said, "He's not your Pa, or your Grandpa." From then on she told us we were to call him "Mr. Miliam." Yet we all just went on as before.

Mr. Miliam built a log cabin for Grandma a few hundred feet from his clapboard house, on the sixty-eight acres he owned in Yak. He even built a walkway between the two houses so he could go see Grandma without getting his boots muddy. Now, this kind of arrangement was unusual between a white man and a colored woman. More common was when a white man had a white wife and a colored mistress on the side. But James Miliam had no white wife, and was entirely devoted to Grandma. They weren't legally married but they lived like man and wife for fifty years and didn't part until death.

They clearly loved each other very much. If anyone was bothered by this relationship, they kept it to themselves. That's because Mr. Miliam was one tough fella, and that's no lie. He was about six feet, four inches at a time when most men were about a foot shorter. When he was a very young man, he had a job rolling huge hogsheads full of tobacco from the countryside to Richmond. Usually, it took two men to roll the barrel. But James Miliam could roll one by himself. All of his adult life, he carried a pistol in a shoulder holster, for all the world to see. He was a mean-looking dude.

That was a time when a colored woman wasn't safe in the least. Men could do anything to a colored woman and they wouldn't get in trouble with the law, not one bit. Well, James Miliam let the word out that if anyone messed with his ladylove, why, he'd track 'em down and blow their head off, and everyone in Pittsylvania County knew he meant it. So, Grandma could come and go as she pleased and no man, colored or white, would tangle with her. No, sir!

Every Sunday, Grandma would walk to the White Rock Baptist Church for services. One time, there was a movement in the church to throw her out, on account of her relationship with Mr. Miliam. But one of the deacons stood up and defended her. He reminded the congregation that those two would have been legally married if they could. And that those two were committed to each other, much more so than some of those in the church that were legally married! And anyway, James Miliam couldn't help being white. So, they let Grandma keep coming to that church.

Mr. Miliam was a farmer, and grew tobacco and everything else you can think of on his land. But he also served as a "dentist." Of course he had no training. It's just that he owned the right tools and was willing to pull teeth. Mr. Miliam would get the two biggest men he could find to hold down the patient, and then he'd yank that old tooth right out. Folks said you wouldn't go to Mr. Miliam unless your tooth ached so bad you wished you were dead anyway.

Another thing: Mr. Miliam was a root doctor. He was always messing around with different herbs and roots and things, looking for cures. As an old man, he got a patent for a cure for scrofula, which was a nasty skin problem that erupted on the necks of folks who had syphilis. Mr. Miliam got $2,500 for the patent. We remember that he went to Richmond to sign the papers, and demanded to be paid in cash. Seems he could not read or write — but he could count cash, yes, sir! He took the train back to Danville, and by then the bank was closed. So he walked the seven miles to Yak with that cash on him, and everybody knew it, too. But nobody bothered him. When he got home, he put that money in a sock and tossed it into the smokehouse, and Grandma said, "What are you doing that for, Jim?" And he said, "Aw, ain't nobody going to bother it. I'll take it to the bank tomorrow." Nobody messed with Mr. Miliam.

Grandma was quite a businesswoman in her own right. She owned her own cow, and although she didn't know it, what she was doing was pasteurizing the milk and cheese. She had somehow discovered that if she scalded her pans with boiling water, the milk and cheese was healthier. She also let the dairy products sit in direct sunlight for a spell. Folks came from all over that part of Virginia to buy Martha Logan's cheese, because it tasted good and lasted longer.

Grandma always had money of her own, and she would give some to us once in a while. She made a garter which she wore on her thigh, and in it she kept five twenty-dollar gold pieces. Grandma always said she liked being able to get her hands on a hundred dollars in a hurry. It was like her social security!

Grandma and Mr. Miliam had two daughters: Eliza, born in 1859 and named after Grandma's mother, and Nanny James, our Mama, born two years later, on June 23, 1861. Mama was named after Mr. Miliam's mother (Nanny) and himself (James). Mr. Miliam's daughters could not carry his last name legally, but he was determined that his name be in there someplace.

Eliza got married young, but Nanny — our Mama — was set on getting an education. She had been inspired, at the little one-room schoolhouse, by a teacher named Miss Fannie Coles. Nanny admired Miss Fannie Coles so much that she would take her own lunch and give it to Miss Coles every day as a gift. Miss Coles had no idea that her student was sacrificing her own meal.

Mama always said she had a sweet childhood there in Yak, carefree and running around the farm, playing with her sister. She was sheltered from the world, though, and when she set her sights on going to Saint Augustine's School in Raleigh, North Carolina, Grandma declared she could not go alone. So when Mama packed her bags, so did Grandma.

The whole time Mama was in college in Raleigh, Grandma was nearby. Grandma was an excellent cook and seamstress and was able to get as much work as she wanted.

Grandma went home to Danville by train as often as she could. When she'd get to the station in Danville, she would tell the boy working there, "Go and tell Jim Miliam that I have arrived and to hurry up and come get me." That boy would rush off to Yak, and Mr. Miliam would just drop what he was doing and hurry all the way to Danville with his mules hitched to the wagon. Grandma was the boss! And they say folks found it amusing to see this colored woman just bossing around the fiercest-looking white man in Pittsylvania County.

Grandma suffered terribly from rheumatism. One day, she told Mama, "Soon my time to die will be coming." She was sixty-six when she died in 1908, which was old in those days. Mama found all her clothes for the funeral pressed and ready, laid out in a drawer. Poor Mr. Miliam, he sat in Grandma's kitchen with his head in his big hands and he said, "What I loved most in this world is lying in the other room."

Before Grandma died she had told Mama to have some of us grandchildren stay with Mr. Miliam when we could because he would be lonely. So we came from Raleigh and cooked and kept him company. In the morning, he would go out and shoot a squirrel for his breakfast. He always used to say those little ones were mighty tasty.

At one point, Mama hired an old lady to do housekeeping for Mr. Miliam, but that didn't work out, because the old woman was hooked on laudanum and would sleep for days at a time. So Mama sent Harry, one of our little brothers, to help out, and he stayed for almost two years. One of Mr. Miliam's white friends almost lost his life for insulting little Harry. This white fella came to dinner and was appalled — just appalled — that this nigger child was to eat with them. One thing colored people and white people did not do was eat at the same table together. The man suggested that Harry eat in the other room, and Mr. Miliam slammed his fist on the table, according to Harry, and said, "Like hell he will! He is my grandson!" And Mr. Miliam told his white friend to get out of his house or he might soon find himself dead and shoveling coal for the Devil.

Grandma had predicted Mr. Miliam would not last long without her, and she was right. Despite our efforts to keep him happy, he died just two years later, in 1910. He was about seventy years old. (He told us he had somehow lost track of his birth date, but he believed he was born in 1840.) Before they buried him, Mama had a decision to make concerning that pistol he always carried with him. Seems everybody in Pittsylvania County coveted that pistol, and all kinds of folks stepped forward and asked to buy it. Mama's own sons, our six brothers, had their eyes on it, too. Someone suggested that Mama just bury it with old Mr. Miliam, and be done with it, and that's what she did. Well, what happened next was this: Somebody went in there and robbed that grave. Dug him up! And when they couldn't get the gun loose from that holster, they just tore his whole arm right off in order to get that gun. It just about broke Mama's heart.

They weren't supposed to be together in life, but Martha Logan and James Miliam are buried together, side by side. Eliza, Mama's sister, had died, and so Mama was the only surviving child. Mr. Miliam left everything he had — his farm and his money from the patent — to her. The will was challenged by some white nephew of his who was just furious over the fact that this *colored* woman should get that land and that money, even if she was Mr. Miliam's daughter! Mama gave $500 to the nephew to keep the fellow happy. She didn't want to be sued. But she did what Mr. Miliam would have wanted: She hung onto that land. And to this day, it is still in our family.

PART III
SAINT AUG'S

In the decades after the Civil War, "education" became the rallying cry of those seeking to improve the lot of former slaves, whose prospects were limited usually to hard labor in the fields or to domestic work in white people's homes. Black people during this era would be lucky to have had the chance to learn to read and write well enough to sign their own names.

To the small but growing black middle class, it was clear that higher aspirations were unattainable without access to higher education. The few black students groomed for advancement found colleges and universities unwelcoming. Indeed, most institutions frankly barred them from admittance. Many white people clung to the belief that black people were incapable of being educated. In the black community, many argued that a classical education was a waste of time for people who had little hope of a future in which to use it. Black women faced even higher hurdles. At a time when most women were expected to marry and become mothers, higher education for them was deemed unnecessary.

Black colleges were the crucial stepping-stone to progress, and they flourished. Northern philanthropists had established, among others, Howard University in Washington, D.C.; Fisk University in Nashville, Tennessee; and Shaw University in Raleigh, North Carolina. Schools for Negroes stressing vocational training, such as the Hampton Normal and Industrial Institute in Virginia and the Tuskegee Institute in Alabama, were also founded with aid from private resources. At the same time, black colleges were started under the auspices of religious organizations, such as the Episcopal Church. Such was the origin of Saint Augustine's School (now College) in Raleigh, founded in 1867.

There are more than one hundred predominantly black colleges still in existence, and of that number forty-eight are private institutions like Saint Augustine's. Many of the schools, particularly public institutions, are rethinking their mission because predominantly white schools today admit — even seek out — black students. Some educators argue that black colleges offer a supportive culture that is invaluable. The debate is ongoing, but for more than a century, black colleges have provided the foundation for achievement in the African-American community. Growing up at Saint Augustine's School, the Delanys learned to "reach high."

7

SADIE AND BESSIE

Our Mama was always a bit embarrassed that her parents were not — could not have been — legally married. She was determined that she was going to have a legal marriage someday, or not get married at all! Virginia was a much more conservative state about these things than North Carolina, and that may have figured into her decision to go to college at Saint Aug's, in Raleigh, and leave Virginia behind.

She got her pick of beaus at Saint Aug's, and it didn't matter to her in the least that her favorite was a lot darker than she was. Some colored women who were as light as Mama would not have gotten involved with a dark-skinned man, but Mama didn't care. She said he was the cream of the crop, a man of the highest quality. Oh, Mama was a smart woman. It takes a smart woman to fall in love with a good man.

Our Papa felt the same way about her, but he was told at graduation time by his advisers that he should not marry, at least not yet. Now that he was educated, they hoped to see him devote himself to the ministry before starting a family. But Papa ignored this advice. He never looked for a fight, but he always managed to do what he wanted, in such a pleasant way that folks could not get mad at him. He took the train home to Fernandina Beach, Florida, after graduation and told his parents he had met the woman he wanted to marry. They presented him with an illustrated Bible in which he wrote: "Given to Henry Beard Delany by his parents upon graduating from college." Then, he took the train back to Raleigh and he and Miss Logan were married at the chapel at Saint Aug's on the sixth of October 1886.

Lemuel Thackara Delany, their firstborn, arrived the next year, on September 12, 1887. He was named after the white Episcopal priest who helped Papa go to college. Every two years after Lemuel's birth, there was a new baby: Sadie in 1889, Bessie in 1891, Julia Emery in 1893, Henry Jr. (Harry) in 1895, Lucius in 1897, William Manross in 1899, Hubert Thomas in 1901, Laura Edith in 1903, and Samuel Ray in 1906. Laura is the only one besides us that is still living. She is our baby sister and lives in California. All of our brothers and our sister Julia have gone on to Glory.

Every child was named for somebody. Sadie (Sarah Louise) was named for her two grandmas. And Bessie (Annie Elizabeth) was named for Dr.

Anna J. Cooper.* Our parents counted Dr. Cooper as a close family friend, and she was known to them as Annie. They met when Dr. Cooper was a teacher at Saint Augustine's School.

When Saint Aug's was founded after the Civil War, it was both a seminary and a school for teachers. A family by the name of Smedes founded Saint Aug's as a school for Negroes and another Episcopal school for whites, Saint Mary's, on the other side of town. Mama remembered one of the Smedes brothers. She said he used to ride up to the school on his horse, and he would get down and take off his hat and bow to the ground at the feet of the students at Saint Aug's, with his hat almost touching the ground. Mama said it was a strange sight, a white man bowing to these colored students!

Many fine, young colored people graduated from Saint Aug's and went on to share what they had learned with countless others. Growing up in this atmosphere, among three hundred or so college students, reading and writing and thinking was as natural for us as sleeping and eating. We had a blessed childhood, which was unusual in those days for colored children. It was the rare child that got such schooling!

* Dr. Anna J. Cooper (1858–1964) was an educator and early advocate of higher education for black women. She was a graduate of St. Augustine's School and Oberlin College, and received a doctorate from the University of Paris in 1925. She received national recognition for her work as principal of M Street High School, for years the only academic high school for Negroes in Washington, D.C.

But since we were girls, our every move was chaperoned. All little girls and young women were chaperoned in those days. That's because things hadn't improved much since slavery days as far as the right of colored women and girls to be unmolested. If something bad had been done to us, and our Papa had complained, they'd have hung *him*. That's the way it was.

Our family lived right on the campus. We were not allowed to go off the campus without an escort. Matter of fact, we were not allowed to go to certain places *on* the campus without someone to go with us. If it wasn't our Mama or Papa, the escort was one of the teachers at Saint Aug's or very often Papa's Cousin Laura from Florida. Papa called Cousin Laura, "Cousin Lot." As children, we shortened that to "Culot."

Poor Culot was a seamstress who had had a miserable job in Florida, working for some white lady. The white lady made a lot of money, and Culot got next to nothing and did all the work. You know, one of those deals. So, Culot had joined up with a convent in Baltimore, but left when she found out that the way those sisters raised money was to beg in the streets. She couldn't stand it. So our Papa got her a job teaching sewing at Saint Aug's, where she stayed until she was a very old woman, when she went back to Fernandina to die. She never worked for white folks again.

Culot took her job as our escort very, very seriously. She looked after us like an old watchdog, and Lord help anyone who came near us. We used to work in the fields that belonged to the school and chop cotton to make a little money for ourselves, and Culot would be sitting under a tree, with one eye on her sewing and the other eye on us — at the same time, yes, sir!

The farm on the campus of Saint Aug's provided food for the staff and students, and it also gave the poorest students a way to pay their tuition and expenses because they could work in the fields and get paid a small amount. Every free chance we got, we worked in those fields to get a little money. Sometimes, they couldn't pay us, because they ran out of money at the school.

Of the two of us, Bessie was the champion cotton-picker. Sadie could pick one hundred pounds of cotton in a day as a teenager, which was a most respectable amount, but Bessie could pick two hundred pounds, which was more than most men. It didn't take brute strength to pick cotton. Women were generally faster pickers than men, especially if they were wiry and agile like Bessie.

Culot was a maiden lady with no children of her own, and she liked to spoil us sometimes, so she would take us on the trolley car to Johnson's drugstore for a limeade, or bring back some candy when she went downtown by herself. Funny thing about Culot is that she never could make a decision. She would tell us, now clean out my dresser drawer and throw most of it out while I am downtown, but *don't ever tell me what you threw away.* And we'd do it. She just couldn't stand to throw anything away herself. A lot of former slaves were like that — they'd never owned anything, so they hung on to all kinds of junk they didn't know what to do with.

Of course, there were many people still alive then who had been slaves — including our Papa. Most of these former slaves were down on their luck. Papa used to say that they didn't know how to live free, especially the ones that had been treated badly. Our parents thought it was their responsibility to treat these former slaves with courtesy and kindness, and with the dignity those folks had been denied by others.

There was an old man named Mr. Holloway, a former slave who lived alone in an abandoned house nearby, and Mama always sent us over there to check up on him. Every Sunday, we shared our dessert with him. Mama would pack up cake and whipped cream, and several of us children would bring it to him, just to be neighborly.

And there was "Aunt" Sukey. She was better off than many former slaves, because when freedom came, her master gave her a cabin on a little patch of land, just off our campus. Aunt Sukey kept to herself, but she seemed mighty happy fussing with her garden. On Sundays, we would walk past her cabin and she'd be outside, and Papa would tip his hat and say, "Mornin', Aunt Sukey."

At Thanksgiving, Papa made sure everybody in the neighborhood around Saint Aug's got a special meal. He would start weeks ahead making the baskets, and finding out who might need one. Then Mama and the girls at the school made sweet potato pies, and vegetables and chicken. (Turkey was a big luxury, and no one ate it, except Grandma up in Virginia, because Mr. Miliam would go out and shoot a wild one for her.) On Thanksgiving morning, it was our job to go out and distribute the baskets. One year, a woman said to Bessie, "Honey child, there ain't a crumb in my house to eat, and I been on my knees praying for Thanksgiving for my chillun. When you got to my house, Thanksgiving surely got here!"

Hunger was a big problem for the former slaves all year long. It always seemed like somebody was knocking on the door, looking for food. Mama never turned anyone away. She'd stop whatever she was doing and fix them a plate. Most of these folks just went on their way, though one, a man named Jesse Edwards, stayed for ten years, until the day he died, living in an abandoned farmhouse on campus. We always called him Uncle Jesse, and he became like a part of our family.

Uncle Jesse had been a slave in Scotland Neck, North Carolina. Papa felt sorry for him, and gave him the job of carrying the mail. Uncle Jesse took this job so seriously that no matter how much we begged, he would not let us see the day's mail, and he'd say, "No, can't do it cuz Mr. Delany said don't give no one dat mail! And dat's dat!"

Mama saw to it that Uncle Jesse got fed three meals a day at the school dining hall. That old fella never had it so good. On Sundays, he attended Baptist Church services downtown, and couldn't get back in time for the noon meal on campus.

He got so spoiled that at breakfast on Sundays he would say, "I would like to take my dinner with me now, if you don't mind." Mama thought that was kind of funny, but she didn't let him know that. She just made arrangements for him to get a plate of yams or whatever else was already cooking for dinner.

As poor Uncle Jesse got older — no one knew how old he was, and he could only guess — he got a little scrappy. Sometimes, we would have to go to his old farmhouse and clean it out, and it was just full of junk. Sometimes, we'd have to cut his fingernails and toenails for him, just generally clean him up and make him presentable.

One day Uncle Jesse got sick, and Papa took him to the hospital, but there was nothing could be done, and poor Uncle Jesse died four days later. We had a potter's field on the campus, where Papa used to bury all the colored people in the area whose folks had no money, and Papa found an especially nice spot for Uncle Jesse's final resting place.

Our potter's field was very different from the white cemetery, which was just across a stream, behind some trees. The white folks' resting place was called the Oakwood Cemetery. Once, they buried a young man who had just been killed in the Spanish-American War, and the mayor was there, and the governor. The people sang, "Free as a Bird to the Mountain." There was a large crowd, standing around the marble headstones and statues. We were so impressed by that cemetery.

Why, the white people even had their names carved into stone! Those white folks sure had money, and they sure went out in style.

Uncle Jesse had a different kind of funeral, but in the Lord's eyes, maybe it was just as good as any white person's — maybe better! We were the chief mourners, along with our little sister Julia. We picked wildflowers and wove them around a wooden cross. Mr. Hunter, the principal of the school, who was white but a very nice man, donated the coffin he was having made for himself at the school carpentry department. Papa presided over the service as if he was burying the king of England himself. All in all, Uncle Jesse had quite a send-off.

8

SADIE

Mama and Papa were the two busiest people I ever knew, but they always had time for us. They *made* time for us. Once, our baby brother, Sam, shouted, "Mama! Mama! Come quick! Come quick!" Well, Mama thought some disaster had happened and she dropped what she was doing in the kitchen and ran to him. And he said, "Mama, look at that sunset. Hasn't the Lord given us a pretty sunset today?" And the two of them watched the sun go down.

But Mama could also be a strict disciplinarian. My first memory is sitting on her lap, and someone gave me a little box of candy. I was eating a piece, and Mama said, "Now, share some with Lemuel." And I started whining and crying because I didn't want to. Finally, Mama took it from me and just threw it right in the fire. She said, "That will teach you to share next time!"

Maybe she had to be strict, on account of there being ten of us. Some women tried to find ways to prevent pregnancies but in those days there really wasn't anything that worked. Once, a friend of Mama's wrote a letter. It said, "Nanny, if you don't want all those babies, just let me know, and I will tell you how you can try to stop it." Mama was very offended. After she read that letter, she declared, "I want all of my children, every single one!"

She would always say to us, "Anything that happens, you can confide in Mama. Mama loves each child the way God loves His children. Nothing's too bad to tell Mama. Don't ever tell me a lie. It's not necessary, because Mama will understand."

She was really a "working" mother, with a job outside the home, making sure everything ran smoothly at Saint Aug's. After Mama had a baby, I would get a little chair and sit outside their bedroom and say, "You can't go in. Mama needs her rest." It was one of the little jobs I made for myself as a mama's child. You'd be surprised at the people who would want to go in there. My younger brothers and sisters, of course, but also all these college students and various people who needed something. Mama was so loved by all the young folks on that campus that they called her "Mother Delany," and they told her things they wouldn't tell a priest. But I wouldn't let them in. So you see, I was a good little helper.

Still, I just don't know how Mama did it all. Her day always started long before dawn, and every night she bathed each one of us in a tin tub which she had to fill by hand. I used to get so tired waiting for my turn because I was the second-oldest child and she would start with the youngest. I don't know why Mama was so concerned about bathing us every day, except that people used to say that Negroes were dirty people and she may have been trying to combat that image. Well, we must have been the cleanest children anyone ever saw.

After each of us had our bath, we would go into Papa's study where he would read to us from the Bible. He'd only read the stories he thought we should hear. I didn't know there were stories in the Bible about adultery and things of that nature until I was a grown girl. After he read us Bible stories, Papa would see to it that any of us children who had had a fuss that day would make up. He didn't let us go to bed without resolving any conflicts. After Mama and Papa tucked us in, Papa would always check on us later. He used to worry about me because sometimes he'd find me sleeping at the foot of the bed with the moon shining on my face. And he'd cover the window. In the morning, he would say, "Now, Sadie, you must not sleep at the foot of the bed with the moon shining on your face because it will warp your features."

The girls slept in one room, and the boys slept in another, except for Lemuel, the oldest child, who had his own, small room. At first we lived in the Smith Building, but the family grew so large we moved to another building which came to be known on campus as the Delany Cottage.

Papa was the head of the house, though he always made sure that we treated Mama with great respect. All of us children had chores to do, and Papa always saw to it that we did them. As a mama's child, I clung to my mother and was actually like her assistant. I would help Mama can fruits and vegetables, or anything she was doing at the moment. Since I was busy helping Mama, Bessie often would supervise the younger children in the family. Tell you the truth, I think she enjoyed bossing them around more than I would have! The little ones used to complain that a gnat couldn't land on them without Queen Bess knowing about it. Bessie was a little dictator!

Each morning, Papa would make us line up for our "inspection." He'd look us over to see if our shoes were polished, our ears were clean, things like that. He was proud of his children and I think this was just a way for him to convey this. We carried the Delany name and he wanted us to look respectable when we left the house.

After our inspection, the bells would chime at the chapel and Papa would scurry off to run the morning prayer service. We children would go to the service, then off to school on the campus. We attended classes taught by teachers in training at the college. Often there were people in the class who were grown men and women who lived nearby who wanted to learn to read and write. So the school we went to was not a traditional school in that regard. There were people of every age studying together. This seemed normal to us, because we didn't know any different.

I never saw people try harder to improve themselves than these grown men and women wanting to learn to read and write. This was the only chance most of them had ever had to get an education, and they were eager to take advantage of it. These folks, along with many of the neighborhood children who attended our school, were very poor.

Sometimes we Delany children felt the teachers were harder on us. Why, one teacher actually suspended me, but Mama marched down there and got me reinstated the very next morning. I remember the teacher had said that the children should come forward and warm their hands at the stove, and so I did, and I think she was angry because the other children were truly cold, having slept with no heat. Well, I was a little thing and I didn't really understand. I guess the teacher thought I was a little spoiled.

Funny thing is, we Delanys had no money at all. We were perceived as an elite family, since our parents were college-educated and had important jobs. But honestly, money was very tight. We bought all our clothes at the mission store and only one time in my childhood do I recall having a new outfit. That was when some white missionaries in New England sent all the Delany children brand-new clothes one Christmas.

None of us had a fancy layette, except Manross. As a baby, he was dressed like a prince. That's because Mrs. Manross, a white teacher at the school who was Mama's good friend, had made an elaborate layette for her baby. But the baby was stillborn, and since Mama was expecting a child, Mrs. Manross just gave her that whole fancy layette. Mama was so flattered by Mrs. Manross's generosity that she and Papa decided to name my little brother after her.

I remember once, Bessie and me and our little sister Julia made a circle around Papa and said, "Papa, we are going to squeeze a nickel out of you!" And he laughed and said, "Go ahead and try, daughters, but there's no nickel here!" But it is really true that you can get by without much money. We had love and respect and all those good things.

Papa was as good a man as you could find in America, or anywhere else for that matter. He was a good father, and we always listened to him, especially after the day Miss Michael flipped over the buggy. Miss Michael was a music teacher at the school and very fond of our little sister Julia, who was very musical, and, in fact, eventually went to Juilliard in New York City. Miss Michael invited little Julia to go for a ride in her new buggy, and Papa said, "Absolutely not. Miss Michael hasn't got any idea what she's doing. Why, she'll flip that thing right over! It's too dangerous."

We begged Papa to let Julia go. We thought he was quite unreasonable, but he would not change his mind. Well, what do you think happened? Miss Michael climbed in her buggy and we watched her go down that dirt road from the school and she lost control of that horse, right before our eyes. The buggy flipped right over. She was not badly injured, but the passenger side where Julia would have been sitting was smashed to bits. This had a great impression on me and Bessie, not to mention Julia. We never doubted Papa again about anything. As far as we were concerned, that man knew everything.

He was highly intelligent, with many interests and hobbies. The one I remember best was astronomy. On a clear night, he would take us all outside and teach us the names of the planets and star constellations. Papa knew them all. I remember that Papa was so excited when Halley's Comet came by. He had us all outside that night, and it was a sight to see, flickering light across the landscape. Papa said, "I don't think any of us will be here to see Halley's Comet the next time it comes around." Well, he was wrong about that, 'cause Bessie and I saw it again and it wasn't as good the second time.

Another thing about Papa: He didn't drink. After Mama had a baby, he would go into town and buy her a lager beer. And he would make her an eggnog, which always involved slipping into his study first, which I realized years later was where he probably put a little whiskey in it. You see, Papa couldn't be much help while the babies were being born. So after the midwife left, he would do these things to help Mama relax, to indulge her a little bit. That was the only time I remember there being liquor in the house.

Papa whipped us once, and only once, when Bessie and I were children. He spotted us in a grove far from where we were supposed to go. We hadn't snuck down there on purpose, we just forgot and kind of wandered down there. Well, Papa was just very upset. He was afraid we could have been molested. I guess we were about six and eight years old. He told us to get switches from the peach tree. While we were doing that I whispered to Bessie, "Now, let's don't cry, no matter how many times he hits us!" Bessie agreed, and volunteered to go first with the whipping. Papa whipped her little shoulders and the backs of her legs, and of course, she did not cry. The whipping went on and on, and she did not cry. Finally, Papa quit and said, "Go on, you stubborn little mule."

Now it came my turn and after seeing what Bessie had gone through I changed my mind about not crying. So I howled at the very first lash, and one lash was all I got. I'm into surviving, and I can see when I'm licked. What's the sense in getting licked if you don't have to?

77

9
BESSIE

Lord, I am still mad at Sadie over that whipping incident! It was her idea not to cry in the first place. Well, I would rather die than back down, and that is the truth.

I take after Mama's people. Mama could be very feisty, and somehow, like me, she lived to tell about it. I remember once how Mama got mad at some white man who wanted to use our telephone. We had a telephone in our house, and that was a very rare thing in those days. The number was 184, and if it rang once, it was for Mr. Hunter, the principal, at his house up the hill, and if it rang twice it was for us. One day, a white man knocked at our door and asked if he could use our phone. He called Mama "auntie," which was one of the put-down ways white people referred to colored people. They'd call men "uncle" or "boy."

Mama told that man, "You may use my phone, but you may not call me auntie. I am no kin to you." Now, that was a very courageous thing for a colored woman to do in those days. Papa would have let it slide.

Papa tended to be gentle and calm. It was not in his nature to be mean or to make a fuss, so it was very difficult for him to whip us that day. And he had a lot of pride. He really believed in presenting yourself to the world in a dignified fashion. I think that's why he was unhappy about my pet pig, Retta. You see, Retta was the runt of the litter, cast aside and left to die. Well, I took that little piglet and I fed him with a bottle and fussed over him like a baby. Before I knew it, he weighed five hundred pounds, and he had these tusks that grew up around his nose. Wherever Sadie and I went, Retta wasn't far behind. I don't think Papa thought it was fitting for a Delany child to be wandering around the campus of Saint Augustine's School followed by a big, grunting bull-pig.

One day, Retta bit a man and that was the end of my poor pig. I imagine he was turned into bacon, and his fat used to make soap. It pains me to this day, because I loved that old pig.

Papa and Mama always taught us to treat animals with respect. You never killed any of God's creatures unless you were going to eat them. Sometimes in the summer Papa and the boys would shoot bull-bats, which I think people now call swallows. Those bull-bats would swarm after the mosquitoes at dusk, just fill the sky, and they'd shoot a dozen or two, and we girls would clean them and we'd eat them for supper. They had a surprising amount of meat on the breast, and tasted mighty good. But Papa would never have let us kill them just for "sport."

All of us knew a thing or two about guns. The boys were all taught to be expert hunters and the girls at least knew the basics of gun safety. But one time our brother Lemuel was carrying a shotgun when a boy tripped him, and Lemuel was shot right through his hand. There were no antibiotics then, of course, and the wound was just full of lead shot and all this corruption just came out of that hole in his hand. Poor Lemuel! Mama sat with him every day while the doctor soaked that hand in hot, hot water. You could hear him scream all the way at the Capitol, a mile away.

Lemuel's hand healed finally, but the accident changed his life. He decided he wanted to be a doctor. One of the white doctors who had healed him took him under his wing. After graduating from Saint Aug's, he studied at Shaw University and then did his internship at the University of Pennsylvania. He returned to Raleigh and became a very well-respected physician. In fact, not long ago, a wing of one of the hospitals there was named in his honor.

We had other calamities besides Lemuel's hunting accident. The worst was a typhoid epidemic when I was about fifteen years old, which was nearly the end of me. A girl named Bessie Jackson, who had it first, died. Then everybody started getting sick. Sadie got walking typhus and was not terribly ill, but I was hospitalized for about six weeks. I remember lying there in that hospital bed and the only thing they'd let me have to eat was albumin water. This was egg white and water, and it was nasty stuff, just nasty! Take my word for it. You see, they believed that typhus would tear up your guts, and that if you ate anything, it would burst your intestines and you would die.

A little girl named Amaza Hill, who was in the bed next to me at the hospital, was recovering more quickly than me. So they gave her a little cornbread. I said, "Amaza, please give me some of that cornbread!" And she said, "Oh Bessie, I can't; I'm afraid you'll die." And she felt so bad she cried. Well I begged her, the one and only time in my life I ever begged for anything. I said, "Amaza, I will never tell a living soul that you gave me a piece of that cornbread." Finally, I wore that girl down and she gave me a tiny piece. I never told anyone, until now. Well, when I ate it, I felt a little better. I swear that girl saved my life.

When I got out of the hospital, I looked like death. They had cut off my hair, real short, and I weighed next to nothing. I could not get enough to eat. Mama was so worried that she fixed a small basket of food each morning for me to carry with me all day, so I could eat whenever I wanted. For a long time I was on crutches, and I was not expected to recover fully. They used to say that typhoid fever left its mark on people. Well, nothing has shown up yet, so I guess I'm in the clear!

Papa and some of the other men believed that

the epidemic was caused by contaminated water. After the epidemic, he installed electricity and plumbing on the whole campus. He was a very handy man.

There were other nasty diseases, too, like malaria and tuberculosis. One fellow on campus came down with smallpox, which was the scariest disease of all. He was isolated immediately. People would leave food for him at a checkpoint, and he would have to get it. It worked, because none of us came down with it.

Mama was real fussy about germs, and also very careful about the foods we ate. She was ahead of her time about vitamins and minerals and things like that. Why, we used to say that Mama invented breakfast cereal. They would make these loaves of bread in huge brick ovens at the school and cut them with a large slicer. Mama would put a pan underneath to scoop up the crumbs, which she'd serve to us in a bowl with milk. People thought it was crazy.

We were very healthy compared to most children of our time. In those days, many babies and children died. They used to say, "There's more short graves in the cemetery than long ones." But Mama didn't lose any of us at birth, and none of us was born damaged.

Our childhood years were so protected, we didn't have but the vaguest notion of what sex was. We had a neighbor who said to us once, "You girls are so green, it's a wonder those cows don't mistake you for grass and gobble you up." I would see the rooster worrying the hen and I didn't know what was happening. But I'd watch the hens and had it figured out when they were just about to pop out an egg. And I'd shout, "Sadie! Sadie! Come quick, if you want to see this hen lay an egg." She kept missing it, so one time I picked up the hen and held her upside down until Sadie got there.

Mama was very private about her pregnancies. When my younger brothers and sisters were born, she would say to me and Sadie, "Now, take the little ones to the grove by the spring and don't come back all day." Well, we'd just sit there quietly all day, and when we'd come back, there would be Miss Kenney, the midwife, and a new little darling colored baby! And we would say, "Mama, where did this baby come from?" And she would point to the midwife and say, "Why, Miss Kenney brought the baby." We thought she meant Miss Kenney brought the baby in her black leather bag.

Sadie was not as curious, but I was very nosy about sex. As a young girl, I would get my hands on a romance novel, which in those days was not very racy. I'd go to the barn, or to the farmhand's house because I knew they couldn't read and wouldn't figure out what I was up to. Well, those old romance novels were silly. You'd get all the way through the book to the sexy part and it would end something like this: "And she swooned, and fell into his arms in a passionate embrace." Now, I ask you, what in the world does that mean?

It wasn't until years later, when I was teaching

school in Brunswick, Georgia, that I finally figured out what this sex stuff was all about from hearing the other teachers talking rather explicitly. They were saying this and that about men, and I thought, Lord have mercy!

Everyone expected a lot from the Delany children, but like all children, we could be mighty mean, especially to each other. We may have been sheltered and disciplined but we were still capable of misbehaving. Our little sister Julia was deathly afraid of bugs, and I used her fear to keep her in line. If there was a bug in our room at night, I could make Julia do things by threatening to throw that old bug in her bed. Wasn't I mean?

Julia followed us around and got in our way. Sadie and I, being older, preferred to play with each other. We were best friends from Day One. Why, Sadie is in my earliest memory. We used to have these terrific thunderstorms in North Carolina that would scare the life out of you, and my first memory is Papa calling us all inside because a storm was coming. We all sat on the floor and Papa said, "Just be quiet. Let God do His work." And the storm was crashing all around outside, and lightning was hitting the lightning rods Papa had put on the house. The whole house was just a-trembling. And so were we! When the storm was over, there was the most beautiful rainbow. Papa said, "Look, children, it is a gift from God." Sadie took my hand and we ran outside to get a better look at that rainbow. We were certain God had hung it in the sky, just for us.

We lived a clean life, but Lord, we had a good time. Why, every one of us children played an instrument, and you know as a family we formed a band. We had a small organ, a Mason & Hamlin, which Papa played beautifully. So did Julia, who had a perfect ear, along with our little brother Sam. We had all kinds of instruments, like a flute, a violin, a trombone, and a clarinet. Papa would lead us. We would play marches; all kinds of music that was popular at the time. In the morning, people would walk past our house and say, "Y'all had a party last night." And we'd say, "Wasn't no party! Was just the bunch of us being musical!"

Papa was extremely talented in music. I used to stand nearby and watch him play the piano. When he thought no one was around he would play and sing these old Methodist hymns from his boyhood. Episcopalians did not have hymns like those old Methodists. He'd play "Amazing Grace," things like that. And I didn't realize it at the time, but I think he missed his people down in Fernandina, in Florida. And when he'd play their Methodist hymns, he felt closer to them.

All of the values that made us strong came from the church. It was religious faith that formed the backbone of the Delany family. We were good Christians, and God never let us down.

I'll tell you something else, honey. We were good citizens, good Americans! We loved our country, even though it didn't love us back.

PART IV
JIM CROW DAYS

A generation after the end of slavery, freedom for black Americans was still elusive. Strategies were being devised, such as poll taxes, to block black Americans from voting, and a flurry of racial restrictions was coming to be codified as "Jim Crow" laws. The Delany sisters recall the beginning of Jim Crow in North Carolina as "the day that everything changed."

Jim Crow became entrenched in Southern society in 1896, with the Supreme Court ruling in the *Plessy v. Ferguson* case. The case stemmed from an incident in which a Louisiana citizen named Homer Plessy was arrested for refusing to sit in a "colored" railroad car. Mr. Plessy lost on his appeal to the Supreme Court, which sanctioned the establishment of "separate but equal" facilities for blacks and whites.

There had long been segregation by custom, but the Jim Crow laws, named for a minstrel show character, made it legal and official. Under the new laws, black Americans faced separate — and inferior — facilities in every part of society, including schools, public transportation, and hospitals. Even public restrooms and drinking fountains in the South were labeled "Colored" and "Whites Only."

By 1914 every state in the South had passed laws that, in effect, relegated Negroes to a lower status than whites. "We knew we were already second-class citizens," recalls Sadie Delany, "but those Jim Crow laws set it in stone."

It would be decades before Jim Crow would begin to finally unravel. In 1954 the Supreme Court ruled in *Brown v. Board of Education of Topeka, Kansas,* that segregation in the public schools was unconstitutional. The passage of the 1964 Civil Rights Act, the 1965 Voting Rights Act, and the 1968 Fair Housing Act were the final death knell for Jim Crow.

10

SADIE AND BESSIE

America has not ever been able to undo the mess created by those Jim Crow laws.

This is how we remember it: The reason they passed those Jim Crow laws is that powerful white people were getting more and more nervous with the way colored people, after the Civil War, were beginning to get their piece of the pie. Colored people were starting to accumulate some wealth, to vote, to make demands. At that time, many white people didn't think Negroes had souls. They thought we were just like animals. They wanted to believe that.

The pecking order was like this: White men were the most powerful, followed by white women. Colored people were absolutely below them and if you think it was hard for colored men, honey, colored women were on the *bottom*. Yes, sir! Colored women took it from all angles!

You see, a lot of this Jim Crow mess was about sex, about keeping the races separate, so they wouldn't interbreed. Ironically, there were very few white people in those days, especially in the South, who did not have some nigger blood. All these white folks who thought they were above Negroes, well, many of them were not pure white! Some knew it, some didn't. But colored people could always pick them out. Papa used to joke that Negro blood must be superior, it must be strong stuff, 'cause it always showed up! You would see these beautiful white-skinned women with kinky hair, and honey, they got it from *somewhere*. This mixing was so common then that there was a saying among poor whites. They used to say, "Takes a little bit of nigger blood to bring out the beauty."

Some of this race mixing that was going on was left over from slavery days, because white men would often molest their slave women, and those women bore mulatto children. But a lot of this racial mixing, especially after slavery days, was just attraction between people, plain and simple, just like happened in our family, on Mama's side. You know, when people live in close proximity, they can't help but get attracted to each other. Also, a lot of white men turned to colored women for romance because they would get turned down by white women, sometimes even their wives. This was because sex in those days was dangerous, and women weren't so enthusiastic about it. Women died in childbirth; it was all risky business. And there were a lot of arranged marriages among the whites, with no love. So white women, who were more powerful than colored women, would sometimes refuse.

So, this Jim Crow mess was started to keep the races apart, and keep the Negroes down. Now, Mama and Papa knew these laws were coming, of course, but they didn't prepare us. I guess our parents could not find the words to explain it. They did not want to fill us with hatred. They did not want us to become bitter. They wanted us to be children and not carry the troubles of the world on our shoulders.

We encountered Jim Crow laws for the first time on a summer Sunday afternoon. We were about five and seven years old at the time. Mama and Papa used to take us to Pullen Park in Raleigh for picnics, and that particular day, the trolley driver told us to go to the back. We children objected loudly, because we always liked to sit in front, where the breeze would blow your hair. That had been part of the fun for us. But Mama and Papa just gently told us to hush and took us to the back without making a fuss.

When we got to Pullen Park, we found changes there, too. The spring where you got water now had a big wooden sign across the middle. On one side, the word "white" was painted, and on the other, the word "colored." Why, what in the world was all this about? We may have been little children but, honey, we got the message loud and clear. But when nobody was looking, Bessie took the dipper from the white side and drank from it.

On another day, soon afterward, a teacher from Saint Aug's took us to the drugstore for a limeade, which was something we had done hundreds of times. Well, this time, the man behind the counter said, "I can't wait on you." The teacher got very upset. She said, "I can see you not waiting on me, but surely you are not going to deny these young children?" And he said, "Sorry. It's the law."

Funny thing is, the white man who owned that drugstore was married to a white lady, and had a colored family on the side. We know this for a fact, because his colored daughter was a friend of ours. She used to go over to the drugstore and he was real nice to her. This was all a big secret in the white community, but all of us colored folks knew all about it. It was kind of a joke, because you see, that was a very prominent white family. That fella even became the mayor of Raleigh.

Jim Crow made it an even bigger stigma to be colored, and any hope of equality between the races came to a grinding halt. Papa used to say that real equality would come as Negroes became more educated and owned their own land. Negroes had to support each other, he used to say.

So Papa would drag us all the way to Mr. Jones's store to buy groceries, since Mr. Jones was a Negro. It not only was inconvenient to shop at Mr. Jones's, it was more expensive. We used to complain about it, because we passed the A&P on the way. We would say, "Papa, why can't we just shop at the A&P?" And Papa would say, "Mr. Jones needs our money to live on, and the A&P does not. We are buying our economic freedom." So Papa put his money where his mouth was. Papa

94

really had that good old American spirit. He believed in individuality, but at the same time, he was dedicated to the community.

Now, lest you think Papa was some kind of a saint, well, he did have a weakness. He did slip into the A&P now and then and buy that Eight O'Clock Coffee, which he was very partial to. So you see, he wasn't perfect, but Lord, he did try!

11

SADIE

Jim Crow was an ugly, complicated business. Fortunately for Bessie and me, our earliest experiences with whites predated Jim Crow. North Carolina was a fairly liberal state, and Raleigh was a center of education as well as the capital. Raleigh was a good place for a Negro of the South to be living, compared to most places at that time. We remember Raleigh when there were still plenty of Confederate veterans hanging around, some lounging on the steps of the Capitol and others at the Old Soldiers' Home. Those veterans were a lonely bunch, and friendly. They always wanted to talk to anybody who walked by.

So our first experience with whites was very positive. The white missionaries who came to Saint Aug's from New England were darling to us. They gave Bessie and me these beautiful china dolls that probably were very expensive. Those dolls were white, of course. You couldn't get a colored doll like that in those days. Well, I loved mine, just the way it was, but do you know what Bessie did?

She took an artist's palette they had also given us and sat down and mixed the paints until she came up with a shade of brown that matched her skin. Then she painted that white doll's face! None of the white missionaries ever said a word about it. Mama and Papa just smiled.

Those white missionaries and teachers at Saint Aug's were taking a great risk. They were outcasts for helping the Negro race. Bessie and I so admired them that we thought they were perfect human beings. One time, Bessie, who was always nosy, noticed that occasionally the teachers would leave the room, and she asked Papa, "Where are they going to?" It didn't occur to her that they were going to the outhouse. It shocked her that they would need to go there. Papa said, "All people are the same. They came from the same place, and they're going to the same place, and while they're here, they're all doing the same things. The only difference between you and anyone else is that compared to most Negroes you have better training."

There was one white woman in particular, Miss Grace Moseley, who was our favorite. She had come to Saint Aug's to teach, along with her mother, and those two were the cream of the crop, child. They were very fine, cultured women, from a good family and with the best manners and education. Miss Moseley didn't like it that at Saint Aug's the white teachers lived separately from the colored. She wanted to live among us.

Now, every Wednesday evening, Miss Moseley

would invite Bessie and me, and our little sister Julia, to her living quarters. And we would all pile on her bed and she would read us Shakespeare and all the classics. Julia was so little she would fall asleep, but Bessie and I would just snuggle up with Miss Moseley and she would read to us. That is a lovely memory I carry with me, and it makes me smile to this day.

On the way to Miss Moseley's cottage there were wild onions growing along the path, and we would break them off and chew on them. When Papa found out, he scolded us. He said, "Shame on you, going up to Miss Moseley's smelling like an old onion patch." Papa hated onions. Mama loved onions, but she never ate them on account of Papa's attitude.

Knowing people like Miss Moseley and our white grandfather, Mr. Miliam, made this Jim Crow mess seem mighty puzzling. Mama ran into some oddball situations, since people often thought she was white. Once she took me on a visit to see her parents in Virginia. I was a toddler, and I guess this was about 1891, while Mama was expecting Bessie. On the way back, we switched trains in Greensboro, and had to wait for about an hour for the train to Raleigh. Well, this white man started to make conversation with Mama, and he picked me up and threw me in the air. Mama tried to discourage him, but he was the persistent type.

Now, Mama knew that white man would not have played with me if he knew I was colored, and he would not have been friendly with her like that. But what was she supposed to do, stand up and say, "Excuse me, but I'm colored"? So she said nothing. Later, when the train got to Raleigh, that white man was shocked to see this good-looking Negro man — our Papa — jump on the train and squeeze Mama tight. The white man said, "Well, I'll be damned." All the white people laughed at him and he said, "That's OK. I had a good time anyway."

Later, after Jim Crow, there were separate cars for colored people and white people. And there were Pullmans, which colored people could ride if they had enough money, but most of us didn't. Anyway, the Pullman was for interstate travel only, and most Negroes were taking local trains. When Papa became a bishop, he occasionally was encouraged by a friendly conductor to take the Pullman instead of the Jim Crow car. But Papa would say no. He would be amiable about it, though. He would say to the conductor, "That's OK. I want to ride with my people, see how they're doing." And he'd go sit in the Jim Crow car.

Now, after Jim Crow, Mama could have traveled in the white car when she took the train. But she insisted on taking the colored car — the "Jim Crow car" — even though it was dirtier. She wanted to be with her people. But sometimes the conductor would think she was white and would make her sit in the white car!

When Mama and Papa went somewhere by train together, they took the Jim Crow car. People would assume that Mama was colored when they saw she was with Papa. But when Mama was traveling by herself, like when she went to see her parents in Virginia, people assumed she was white.

Jim Crow's not law anymore, but it's still in some people's hearts. I don't let it get to me, though. I just laugh it off, child. I never let prejudice stop me from what I wanted to do in this life.

I'll tell you how I handled white people. There was a shoe store in Raleigh called Heller's. The owner was a Jewish man, very nice. If you were colored, you had to go in the back to try on shoes, and the white people sat in the front. It wasn't Mr. Heller's fault; this was the Jim Crow law. I would go in there and say, "Good morning, Mr. Heller, I would like to try on those shoes in the window." And he would say, "That's fine, Miss Delany, go on and sit in the back." And I would say, "Where, Mr. Heller?" And he would gesture to the back and say, "Back there." And I would say, "Back *where?*"

Well, I'd just worry that man to death. Finally, he'd say, "Just sit anywhere, Miss Delany!" And so I would sit myself down in the white section, and smile.

Now, Bessie thinks that I shouldn't play dumb like that. She says he must've thought I was the dumbest nigger alive. But I don't care. I got to sit in the white section.

When I was a grown woman, after I got my master's degree from Columbia University, there was a white teacher who used to say this about me: "That Sarah Delany. You tell her to do something, she smiles at you, and then she just turns around and does what she wants anyway."

Just like Papa.

12

BESSIE

This race business does get under my skin. I have suffered a lot in my life because of it. If you asked me how I endured it, I would have to say it was because I had a good upbringing. My parents did not encourage me to be bitter. If they had, I'd have been so mean it would have killed my spirit a long, long time ago.

As a child, every time I encountered prejudice — which was rubbed in your face, once segregation started under Jim Crow — I would feel it down to my core. I was not a crying child, except when it came to being treated badly because of my race, like when they wouldn't serve us at the drugstore counter. In those instances, I would go home and sit on my bed and weep and weep and weep, the tears streaming down my face.

Now, Mama would come up and sit on the foot of my bed. She never said a word. She knew what I was feeling. She just did not want to encourage my rage. So my Mama would just sit and look at me while I cried, and it comforted me. I knew that she understood, and that was the most soothing salve.

When I was a child, the words used to describe us most often were colored, Negro, and nigger. I've also been called jiggerboo, pickaninny, coon — you name it, honey. Some of these words are worse than others, and how mean they are depends on who is saying them and why.

There was an attitude among some Negroes that to be lighter-skinned was more desirable. There was a saying: "The blacker the berry, the sweeter the juice. But too much black and it ain't no use." If you were very dark-skinned you were looked down upon, even by other Negro people! I doubt that was true among Negro people back when we were in Africa. It's probably just a cultural thing that Negroes picked up from white people in America. We saw in our own family that people treated the lighter-skinned children better. But it was not something that was even *discussed* in our household. We were different shades, and it didn't make a bit of difference among us. It didn't matter if you were white, black, grizzly, or gray, you were *you*.

I don't use the word black very often to describe myself and my sister. To us, black was a person who was, well, black, and honey, I mean *black as your shoe*. I'm not black, I'm brown! Actually, the best word to describe me, I think, is colored. I am a colored woman or a Negro woman. Either one is OK. People dislike those words now. Today they use this term *African American*. It wouldn't occur to me to use that. I prefer to think of myself as an American, that's all!

You see, I think I'm just as good as anyone. That's the way I was brought up. I'll tell you a secret: I think I'm *better!* Ha! I remember being aware that colored people were supposed to feel inferior. I knew I was a smart little thing, a personality, an individual — a human being! I couldn't understand how people could look at me and not see that, because it sure was obvious to me.

It used to be that you would encounter white people who were very patronizing. In some ways, I disliked them the most. These were the type who thought we were all stupid. Little Negro children, in our day, had to put up with white folks rubbing their hands on your head for good luck. That's right. They thought that if they rubbed the head of a pickaninny, it would bring them luck, like a rabbit's foot, or something like that. So I'd try to keep my head out of reach of white folks, yes, sir.

You know, white people were always looking for good colored maids and mammies. Why, sometimes white people would visit the campus and they would point to Sadie and me, and ask Mama if they could take one or the other of us with them. Mama would bristle. "Those girls are my daughters, and they aren't going anywhere," she would say.

One time, as a girl, I was offered a job by a white lady to live at her house and do some work for her. It was just off campus, not far from home, and I thought, Hmmm, could make a little money. But Mama said, "It is completely out of the question!" I couldn't understand it then, but I do now. Mama did not want us to be maids for white people.

Nobody believes this, but it's true: Neither Sadie nor I ever worked for white people in our entire lives! As a dentist, I had quite a few white patients, and Sadie worked for white principals in schools in New York City, but we never worked for white people in their homes. No, sir, not even once! That is one of the accomplishments in my life of which I am most proud, yes, sir! But there are colored people who say, "Well, how'd you make your money, then?" They simply can't believe it.

Mama and Papa tried to protect us, but the real world was out there, and they couldn't shelter us forever. Papa had his newspapers, and he wouldn't let us see them, but we were nosy children, especially me. My grandpa, Mr. Miliam, used to say to Mama, "Nanny, every one of your children could have been detectives, especially Bessie." It was the truth!

It wasn't long before we learned the worst news imaginable: Colored folks were being murdered. They were being lynched. We would hear the teachers talking among themselves about some poor Negro just walking down the side of the road, in the wrong place, at the wrong time. These rebby boys would just grab him and hang him from a

105

tree, just for fun. It was like entertainment to those fellas.

Pretty much, these rebby boys left us alone at Saint Aug's. You'd think they'd have gone after the uppity darkies at Saint Aug's who were getting an education, but I guess they knew that part of the school was a seminary. We got some protection just by being on the campus, within Raleigh.

But Papa still insisted that my brothers be home by dark and he taught them how to keep out of trouble. You see, sometimes they'd lynch a colored man who objected to being called "uncle," things like that. If a white woman said a colored man had looked at her in a certain way, that was the end of him. The rebby boys would come in the middle of the night, and get him out of his bed and hang him up, in front of his wife and children. Sometimes they'd hang his whole family. Or he'd come home and find his woman hung, as punishment for something he supposedly had done. Why, there was one story I heard of a pregnant colored woman who was hung from her feet, and they slit her abdomen open and let the fetus fall out, and she and her unborn baby just died right there, like that.

Lord have mercy! I do not understand any of this. And it doesn't make any more sense to me now than it did then. If it weren't for those kind white missionaries at Saint Aug's, and my mother's white relatives who loved me, I would have hated all white people. Every last one.

Once in a while, God sends a good white person

my way, even to this day. I think it's God's way of keeping me from becoming too mean. And when he sends a nice one to me, then I have to eat crow. And honey, crow is a tough old bird to eat, let me tell you.

13

SADIE

I sometimes think maybe we were a little too sheltered. Why, I was almost afraid of men, really. I wasn't allowed to go downtown by myself until I was a grown girl, and then I was always kind of jittery.

Once, a white man pulled up to me in a car and asked for directions. Well, I remembered what my Papa always said: "You have no business ever talking to a white man or a married man, colored or white. Those men have nothing good to offer you, do you understand?" Those words kept going through my head, and I just kept on walking. That man sort of followed me, shouting that he needed directions. Finally, the man yelled, "What are you, deaf?!" And I stopped, and I just gave him the directions, and that's all he wanted, after all. But I was scared to death of him!

You can imagine that when it came time for me to graduate from Saint Aug's, I didn't want to leave. That campus was the only home I'd ever known. My brother Lemuel also did not want to go out into the world. When he finished medical school and was fixing to get married, he had this idea he'd move his bride right in with us. But Papa said, "I'm sorry, Lemuel, but you can't live at home once you have a wife. This is your Mama's house. We can't have two queens in one hive."

Papa expected me to leave home, too. At the time I graduated, in 1910, a degree from Saint Aug's qualified you to teach school. Many students went on to four-year colleges from there. Often the seminary students went on to places like Yale University, and some of us who had graduated from the Normal School later went to liberal arts colleges. Now, on graduation day, Papa said to me, "Daughter, you are college material. You owe it to your nation, your race, and yourself to go. And if you don't, then shame on you!"

Well, it seemed to me that I had no choice but to go on with my schooling. But Papa said, "Daughter, I have no money. But you must not take a scholarship. If you take a scholarship, you will be beholden to the people who gave you the money. You must make your own way."

So I started looking for teaching jobs and I found out there was an opening for Jeanes Supervisor, which involved visiting schools all over Wake County, North Carolina. Now, I was not quite twenty-one years old in 1910, which was awfully young to be applying for the position, but I got the job. I remember stepping off the train in Method, North Carolina, for my interview, and the mayor, Mr. O'Kelly, said to me, "For Heaven's sake, Miss Delany, at least put your hair up. You look like a schoolgirl." I was still wearing my hair in plaits.

"Jeanes Supervisors" were called that after a white man named Jeanes who had started a fund to introduce domestic science to colored schools in many parts of the South. The colored schools were far inferior to the white schools. Oftentimes, "school" was held at a church and the children would kneel on the floor and use the pews as desks. There were usually no facilities to teach domestic science so I would borrow someone's kitchen, and once I got a class started, I would hire a teacher to take up where I left off. Now, I was just supposed to be in charge of domestic science, but they made me do the county superintendent's work. So, I ended up actually in charge of all the colored schools in Wake County, North Carolina, although they didn't pay me to do that or give me any credit.

I continued to live at home, because I was able to visit many of these schools on day trips. I would go by train or by horse and buggy. Then my brother Lemuel returned from Philadelphia, where he had done his medical internship, and he had a car — the first one in our family. Papa and Mama didn't like cars, and never learned to drive. When I was a child, there were so few cars in Raleigh that we would drop whatever we were doing when we heard one coming and run to see this rickety-looking thing lurching down the road.

Well, I learned to drive Lemuel's car, and naturally, since I had learned to drive, Bessie decided she needed to learn, too. It seems to me she landed Lemuel's car in a ditch while she was learning! Lemuel wasn't too happy.

I got to be a good driver, and when Mr. Booker T. Washington* would come to visit Raleigh, he would climb into the passenger seat of Lemuel's car and I would drive him all around the county and show him my schools. He was so appreciative of the work I was doing.

I don't think folks appreciate Booker T. Washington today; and even then, more radical Negroes looked down on him because they had higher aspirations for the race than he apparently did. But Mr. Washington tried to help his people by getting them educated, getting their feet on the ground. He helped a lot of people and I don't think we should judge him harshly. He was a great American, a gentleman — a lovely man! He was a very amiable sort of man.

As Jeanes Supervisor, I saw the world as I never had before. At twenty years old, I had only visited

---

* Booker T. Washington (1856–1915) was one of the most influential black leaders in American history. He founded the Tuskegee Institute in Alabama, a school for blacks that stressed vocational training. Washington believed that the best interests of his race were to be gained through education and improved economic status, not political agitation.

two places: Yak, Virginia, where Mama's parents lived, and Fernandina, Florida, when I went to visit my Papa's people. My world consisted of the campus of Saint Aug's and downtown Raleigh. Now I saw for the first time what life was really like for my people. I realized that I was a child of privilege, and that I must share my good fortune. I kept remembering what my Papa always said: "Your mission is to help somebody. Your job is to help people." Yes, those words kept me going.

This was forty-five years after the Surrender, and most of these Negroes were in bad shape, child. It was like the ghetto is today. These people needed help with the basics. They didn't know how to cook, clean, eat properly, or anything! Oftentimes, learning to read and write for the children was not the top priority. Teaching people about food preparation — like how to can food — was more important. Also, they didn't know much about sanitation or hygiene, and the women didn't know how to take care of their newborn babies. I taught them how to take care of the umbilical cord, things like that.

I know that I helped many people as Jeanes Supervisor, and I am very proud of that. I inspired many people to get an education, and quite a few went on to Saint Aug's. A lot of the time, what those folks needed was inspiration, a little encouragement. That goes a long way. They looked up to me, and I showed them it was possible to live a better life, despite what white people were trying to do to us.

It was easy for me to get to know these poor, colored folks well because I often had to stay overnight with a local family when I was too far away to return home. Oh, those were hard times, child! I never complained, but how I would long to be back at my Mama's house on those nights, with electricity and indoor plumbing! Sometimes, the people didn't even have outhouses. They just went into the woods, dug a hole, and covered it up again.

The nicest place to stay was at the O'Kellys' house in Method, an all-colored town three miles outside Raleigh. Everyone was colored, including the people who ran the town, like Mr. O'Kelly. He was the mayor, and he owned a country store, and he was the postmaster. His wife was an excellent housekeeper, who had fine china and a room just to entertain company. At home, we had a parlor, too, but we *used* every room in our house.

One thing about Mrs. O'Kelly, though, is that she had tuberculosis. They used to have to wash her dishes separately from ours, and scald them. I think Mrs. O'Kelly found this insulting. She'd say, "Just use my china plates and throw them out, why don't you." It was true that she had enough china that she probably could have done that. The O'Kellys were very well off.

But poor Mrs. O'Kelly and her daughter both died of tuberculosis eventually. That was a big problem then, and I hear it's becoming a problem again. I used to raise money for tuberculosis patients, who were sent to these places called sanitariums to get better, though a lot of them never came back. There were separate sanitariums for colored people and white people. You know what? The whites used to take the money the colored people raised and give it to the *white* place. They weren't a bit bashful. You weren't supposed to have enough sense to notice.

If Mrs. O'Kelly and her daughter, in their fine house, had tuberculosis, imagine what I was exposed to when I stayed with people in the backwoods. But I never did get sick.

I guess one of the worst places to stay was Knightdale, where they put me up in a place full of bedbugs. Once Bessie came along with me to keep me company, and in the morning she ran her hand across the bed and squashed those little bugs, and there was just a streak of red blood. She was mad as a hornet. She and I had a big fuss. She said, "Sadie, I am going home! I am going to Mama's, where there ain't no bedbugs!" And I said, "Oh Bessie, please don't leave." And she said, "If you're crazy enough to stay somewhere where the bedbugs eat you alive, it's your problem! I'm going home!"

Well, I implored her not to say anything to the woman who owned the house, but of course she did. The woman said, "I hope those bedbugs didn't bother you too much," and Bessie said, "Well, as a matter of fact, they ate us up!" And the woman said, "Nobody's slept there in a while so I guess they were hungry." Of course that made Bessie even more furious because the woman *knew* there were bugs in there. So Bessie left, and I came home to Raleigh the next day. But after that, whenever I had to go back to Knightdale, I made sure I planned it so I didn't stay overnight.

Here I was, traveling around the countryside, a grown woman with professional responsibilities. Yet Papa was still in charge of my social life. He didn't want me to go out with any fresh boys, so he selected my gentlemen friends. When I had a caller, we would sit in the parlor to talk. That was about all we were allowed to do. Papa would sit in the other room and read his newspaper and I am quite sure he was listening to every word.

I had one beau named Frank who was particularly fond of me. He was a fellow student of Lemuel's, studying medicine at Shaw University. Papa used to get kind of annoyed with Frank because he talked too much, and would keep talking even when Papa thought it was time for him to leave. Lights went out at the school at ten o'clock, and Papa couldn't stand the idea of our house still having lights on past that hour. It didn't look good. So one time I remember Papa called to me, and I left Frank in the parlor, and Papa said to me, "Are you going to tell him to leave, or am I?" And I said, "Oh, Papa, I can't tell him to leave! I don't want to hurt his feelings!" So I didn't, and neither did Papa. Instead, Papa just cleared his throat and stomped around, hoping Frank would get the hint. We used to have to practically shove Frank out the door.

Now, I liked Frank a lot, but then one day,

Papa told me, "Sadie, you won't be seeing any more of Frank for now." It seems Lemuel had reported to Papa that Frank had been linked to some scandal involving a young nurse. Well, Frank was never able to clear his name to Lemuel's and Papa's satisfaction. I guess he really was involved somehow but I never learned the details. All I know is that I never saw Frank again.

Well, here I am an old maid. Ooops, I shouldn't say "old maid" 'cause it makes Bessie mad. Bessie says we're "maiden ladies." Well, whatever we are, I have no regrets about it. I think Frank would have worried me to death. I've had a good life, child.

14

BESSIE

I suppose Lemuel and Papa thought they were doing the right thing by Sadie, forbidding her to see Frank anymore, but I don't think it was right. She was a grown woman. She should have had a say. It was her choice to make, not theirs!

Oh, I don't know what she saw in old Frank, anyway. He was kind of dull and he talked too much, though I guess I shouldn't say that, because I can outtalk anyone. Yes, sir! I don't know how Sadie's put up with this old flabbermouth for the past one hundred years.

Don't you go thinking because we are maiden ladies that Sadie and I didn't have lots of beaus. We were popular, good-looking gals, but I think we were too smart, too independent for most men. This was especially true for me when I went to teach in Boardman, North Carolina. Honey, when you get to be one hundred years old, you look back and see things very clearly. And I can see I kind of overwhelmed those boys in Boardman, North Carolina, back in 1911!

After I graduated from Saint Aug's, I got the same speech from Papa that Sadie got — the one about going on to a four-year college, paying my own way, and so on. So I got a job as a teacher, doing the same thing as Sadie: saving money and helping my people.

I was twenty years old, and it was the first time I was away from home by myself. Papa took me to the train station in Raleigh and I put on a brave front. But when that train pulled away from the station and I looked back and saw my Papa standing there, watching me, I thought I was going to die. I started to sob. I cried so hard that the people from the white car came to the colored car to get a look at this little darkey just a-carrying on! Well, I'm embarrassed to say I created quite a commotion. The conductor came along and said, "What's the matter, did somebody die?" Now, what'd he have to go and say that for? It was my girlhood that was dying, and I knew it.

I just kept crying until I was all cried out. Then I wiped up my face and sat up straight for the rest of the trip. I tried to remember what my grandpa, Mr. Miliam, told me about holding your head up high. "Bessie, don't ever be afraid to look somebody in the eye. You're just as good as anybody." Well, I tried to remember that, which was hard, because I had left home for the first time and had just made a fool of myself howling like a baby.

When I got to Boardman, I was completely pulled together. But, honey, I was appalled by the place. It was a nothing town, let me tell you. All the men worked in the lumber mill, and all the people shopped at the company store. I was to stay with a Mr. and Mrs. Atkinson in their home.

It turned out I was the most exciting thing that happened to Boardman, North Carolina, in about a hundred years. Those poor colored folks thought I was *something,* which was a big surprise to me. My students loved me so much they would build a fire in the stove before I arrived at school, and they all fought to carry my lunch and my books, especially the little boys. I don't know why my students loved me so much, because I was a dictator! But the children would follow me home after school and Mrs. Atkinson would have to run them off. She would say, "Now, children, Miss Delany has had to put up with you all day. Let her have a little time to herself. Go on home."

Lord, I helped to raise a lot of children in my life, starting with my own brothers and sisters, and then as a teacher. Mama used to say, "Bessie, you are good at raising children. You ought to marry a farmer and have ten of them and live out in the country." And I said, "No way, Mama! I've gone and raised yours, I don't want any!" I felt like I had raised the world!

Anyway, back to Boardman. Now, the menfolk in that town were just smitten with Miss Bessie Delany. I was pretty and had a nice figure, but looking back I think they were impressed by my self-confidence and the way I carried myself. Papa didn't call me Queen Bess for nothing! I was an educated girl from Raleigh, the daughter of an Episcopal priest. Mrs. Atkinson would say, "Child, they've never seen the likes of you."

I remember walking through that town and the colored men would just stop and stare. They wouldn't say a word, they'd just take off their hats when I walked by. One time, I passed by several men and I turned and said, *"Just what are you looking at?"* They didn't answer. Finally, one of them said, "Why, Miss Delany, we can't help it; you look just like a slice of Heaven." And I said, "Well, I ain't *your* slice of Heaven, so put your eyes back in yo' *head*." Honey, I meant business.

When it came to men, I never gave them an inch. I never gave them a quarter of an inch! And all the men knew it. Not for money or nothin' else! No, sir!

But it could get mighty lonely. The whole time I was in Boardman — from 1911 to 1913 — I had but a single caller. One day Mrs. Atkinson said to me, "Miss Delany, a young man from the mill would like to pay a call on you." And I said, "Well, that would be all right."

So he came by and we sat in the little front room of the Atkinsons' house, while the Atkinsons sat in their bedroom, listening. My visitor was a sawed-off little fella. I was five feet, seven inches of height, and unfortunately for him, I like my men *tall*. We chatted for a while. I remember telling him that history was my favorite subject at Saint Aug's. This poor fella probably had a fourth-grade education at best, and there I was yammering about Raleigh and the Saint Aug's campus. Well, he never came by again.

Life was hard for me in Boardman. The room I slept in at the Atkinsons' house belonged to their only child, who had died. There was a great big photo of him over the bed. It made me feel kind of sad.

On my first night there, I said to Mrs. Atkinson, "I would like to take my bath now, please." I figured I'd have to bathe in a tin tub in the kitchen. That's what most folks did, those who didn't have nice plumbing. Well, I went into my room to change and she knocked on the door. I opened it and she handed me a pitcher and a bowl of water. That was it! That was how I was supposed to take my bath! Well, I learned you can bathe pretty well that way. You can get mighty clean, but it takes a while. This was a bit of a shock for Miss Bessie Delany of Raleigh, though.

Mr. Atkinson was the ugliest man I ever saw, and not at all well educated, but he was an absolute gentleman. He never bothered me once. His first name was Spudge, which was short for Spudgeon, or so he told me. He said he was named after a Baptist preacher who was legendary in those parts, and he was just appalled that this little Episcopalian girl had never heard of him.

There was no Episcopal Church in Boardman, so I attended Baptist or Methodist services. They were poor and had no hymnals. The Methodists had the words to their hymns scratched out in the margins of old pieces of paper, like the Sears catalog.

The food we ate in Boardman was about the worst diet I have ever been on. I have always been a slim thing, but honey, I got fat while I was there! When I came home at Christmas I weighed 153 pounds and people came from everywhere to see this fat Bessie. But I lost that weight eventually, and never gained it back. Sadie says it was from eating all that fatback and collards and sweet potatoes in Boardman.

Those people didn't know the first thing about vitamins or minerals. They were so poor and ignorant. It was the same thing Sadie was running into as Jeanes Supervisor in Wake County. Mama was worried about me, and she would send me these little care packages. She would go to a store in Raleigh called the California Fruit Company, and buy some grapefruits and ship them to me.

Well, Mr. Spudge Atkinson had never seen a grapefruit before. He said, "Miss Delany, what is that ugly-looking piece of fruit?" Now, I gave him a piece and he just puckered up and spit it out and said it was the worst, most sour, miserable thing he'd ever put in his mouth! And I said, "Mr. Atkinson, if you're just going to waste my grapefruit, then please give it back to me." And he gave me the rest back, gladly. He sure did think that Miss Delany from Raleigh was peculiar, sitting on his porch sucking down grapefruit.

Mr. Atkinson tended to be a rather dramatic man. One time he came into my classroom and said, "Oh, Miss Delany! Miss Delany!" And I said, "What's the matter, Mr. Atkinson?" And he fell to the ground and said, "It's terrible, it's just terrible!" And I said, "What's terrible?" And he said, "That ship they said could not sink, well, it's done sunk! And all those rich white people have gone down with it, in that icy water!"

I didn't say it out loud, but I remember thinking, Too bad the *Titanic* didn't take more rich white people down with it, to its watery grave! Especially some of the rebby boys around here! Now, isn't that awful of me? Isn't it vicious? You see why this child is worried about getting into Heaven? Sadie is just shocked by me sometimes. Sadie just says, "Live and let live."

But in a way, I was a sweet child, too. You know, when I was in Boardman and got my first paycheck — $40 a month — I paid nine dollars for my room and board and sent the rest home to Papa immediately. No one had asked me to do that. It just seemed like the right thing to do.

Well, I got a letter back from Mama. She thanked me for the money but she told me not to send any more. She told me to save it for myself, or I'd never get to college.

I saved most of my money, but I will admit that I spent some on a silk dress, yes, sir! Papa wouldn't let me have a silk dress, I guess because it was so expensive but also kind of sexy. So, when I was in Boardman I ordered several yards of silk. I think it was blue, with a thin white stripe. And I made myself a dress. Skirts were going up, and you could see the ankle when you walked. And when the men would see a glimpse

123

of ankle they would say, "Oooooh-weeee!" Papa didn't like that at all. When Sadie and I would wear those dresses, he would just scowl at us! Today women show everything. They're crazy. Trust me, you can get in enough trouble just with a little ankle showing.

Now, after two years in Boardman, it was time for me to move on to a new teaching assignment. The people didn't want to see me go, but I was ready for a new challenge. So in 1913 I went to Brunswick, Georgia, to teach at Saint Athanasius School, an Episcopal school for colored children. I wanted to see the world!

Brunswick was a sophisticated place compared to Boardman. The faculty lived together in a dormitory, and that is how I met my lifelong friend, Elizabeth Gooch. "Gooch," as I always called her, was the oldest one of us, and I was the youngest, and so the principal assigned the two of us to room together. I guess he thought Gooch would be a good influence on me, but I think I was a good influence on Gooch!

I didn't like Gooch that much at first. She didn't treat me the way I would have liked to have been treated. For instance, she took the bed away from the window, so that I'd get the draft at night. But after a while, Gooch and I became good friends. Sometimes, we'd go to the beach and see the turtles come in from the sea to nest.

Now, Georgia was a mean place — meaner than North Carolina. You know that song about Georgia, that sentimental song? Well, they can have it! They can have the whole state as far as I'm concerned.

In Georgia, they never missed a chance to keep you down. If you were colored and you tried on a hat or a pair of shoes, honey, you owned 'em. What a rebby state! To be fair, I can understand why they didn't want Negroes to try on hats without buying them because in those days, Negroes would grease their hair. And the store couldn't sell the hat if it got grease on it. So, to be fair, I think that was OK.

But it was on my way to my job in Brunswick in 1913 that I came close to being lynched. You see, I had to change trains in Waycross, Georgia. I was sitting in the little colored waiting room at the station, and I took my hair down and was combing it. I was fixing myself up. I was going to my new job, and I wanted to look nice.

Well, there I was with my long hair down when this white man opened the door to the colored waiting room. There was no one in there except me and two colored teachers from New York who were traveling with me to Brunswick. The white man stuck his head in and started, well, leering at me. He was drunk, and he smelled bad, and he started mumbling things. And I said, "Oh, why don't you shut up and go wait with your own kind in the white waiting room?"

What happened next was kind of like an explosion. He slammed the door and I could hear him shouting at the top of his lungs outside, "The nigger bitch insulted me! The nigger bitch insulted me!"

125

The two colored teachers traveling with me slipped out the back without a word and made a beeline for the woods. They hid in the woods! I guess I can't blame them. A colored porter came in to see what this was all about, and he whispered to me, "Good for you!" But then he ran out on me, too. He left me there by myself.

Well, I could see a crowd begin to gather on the platform, and I knew I was in big trouble. Papa always said, "If you see a crowd, you go the other way. Don't even hang around long enough to find out what it's about!" Now, this crowd was outside, gathering for *me.*

By now, there were dozens of white people in the crowd, and the white man kept yelling, "Nigger bitch insulted me!" I was just waiting for somebody to get a rope. Thousands of Negroes had been lynched for far less than what I had just done. But I just continued to sit on the bench, combing my hair, while that white man was a-carrying on! I realized that my best chance was to act like nothing was happening. You see, if you acted real scared, sometimes that spurred them on.

Two things saved me: That glorious, blessed train rounded the bend, breaking up the crowd and giving me my way to get on out of there. And it helped that the white man was drunk as a skunk, and that turned off some of the white people.

But I wasn't afraid to die! I know you ain't got to die but once, and it seemed as good a reason to die as any. I was ready. Lord, help me, I was ready.

You know what Sadie says? Sadie says I was a fool to provoke that white man. As if I provoked *him!* Honey, he provoked *me!* Sadie says she would have *ignored* him. I say, how do you ignore some drunk, smelly white man treating you like trash? She says, child, it's better to put up with it, and live to tell about it. She says at the very least I should have run off into the woods with those other two teachers. She says I am lucky to be alive. But I would rather die than back down, honey.

Sadie Delany as an
infant, about 1890

Bessie Delany as an
infant, about 1892

(Top left): Jordan Motley, our Mama's grandfather, who was born around 1810
(Bottom left): Eliza Logan, our Mama's grandmother, who was born around 1812
(Top right): Martha Logan, our Mama's mother, as a young woman, about 1860
(Bottom right): James Miliam, our Mama's father, in the late 1850s. He was said to be the meanest-looking man in Pittsylvania County, Virginia.

Thomas Sterling
Delany, our Papa's
father.

Sarah, our Papa's
mother, a slave who
was part American
Indian.

(Top): The Delany family around 1898. Sadie is standing at left; Bessie is seated on the floor at her feet.

(Left): "Culot," our chaperone, around 1906. Her real name was Laura E. Beard.

(Right): Sadie studying Greek at Saint Augustine's School under the tutelage of Professor Charles Boyer, 1908.

Our Mama, second from left, teaching a cooking class at Saint Augustine's School, about 1905.

The Delany family, about 1905, in front of the Delany cottage on the campus. Standing, from left are Papa, Sadie, Harry, Mama (holding baby Sam), Julia, and Lemuel. Seated or kneeling, from left are Lucius with the family dog, Pax, Manross, and Bessie, holding Laura. Hubert is standing between Papa and Mama.

Bessie, left, with our sister, Julia, and a friend of Sadie's, Rayford Lightner, cutting up on a Sunday afternoon, about 1919.

Bessie in her classroom in Brunswick, Georgia, in 1914. It was on the way to her teaching job in Brunswick that Bessie was nearly lynched.

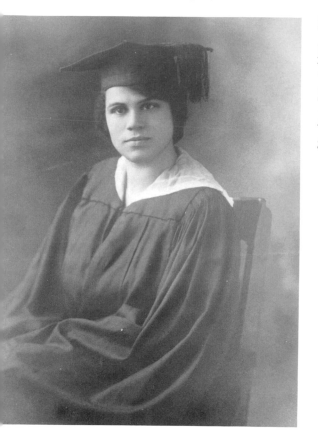

Sadie's graduation photograph, Columbia University, 1920. She later earned a Master's in Education at Columbia in 1925.

Bessie's yearbook photograph, Columbia University, 1923. Upon earning a Doctor of Dental Surgery Degree, she became the second woman licensed to practice dentistry in New York.

The Delany family on a Harlem rooftop. This
was the last family photograph before Papa's
death in 1928. Standing, from left are Manross,
Lucius, Hubert, Harry (Hap), Sam, and
Lemuel. Seated, from left are Julia, Sadie, Papa,
Mama, Bessie, and Laura.

(Above): Mama and Sadie, center, in St. Mark's Square, Venice, in 1930.
(Right): Bessie at Atlantic City in the early 1930s.

Bessie holding our
nephew, "Little
Hubie," on a
Sunday outing
on Long Island
in 1934.

Hubert Delany, as
he appeared on the
cover of *The Crisis*,
the influential
publication
produced by
the N.A.A.C.P.

The Delany family in a World War II-era
photograph. Seated, from left, are Bessie, Mama
and Sadie.

Bessie at age 100. Sadie at age 102.

Bessie, center, and Sadie, right, visiting out
longtime friend Elizabeth Gooch in Covington,
Kentucky, in the late 1950s. "Gooch" had been
Bessie's friend and roomate in Brunswick,
Georgia, in 1914.

PART V
HARLEM-TOWN

Harlem in its heyday of the 1920s and early 1930s was the spiritual center of black America and the birthplace of a vibrant culture that came to be celebrated as the Harlem Renaissance. Writers such as Langston Hughes, Zora Neale Hurston, James Weldon Johnson, Jean Toomer, and Countee Cullen were creating the first substantial body of literature to chart the current of black life. Jazz — America's unique musical voice — was in full flower, and Harlem was the showcase for such pioneering composers and performers as Ferdinand "Jelly Roll" Morton, Louis Armstrong, Bessie Smith, Fletcher Henderson, and Edward Kennedy "Duke" Ellington.

The creative ferment of the Jazz Age made Harlem the undisputed capital of nightlife not just in New York, but for all of America. Among its famous night spots were the Lenox Club, the Bamboo Inn, the Plantation Club, the Clam House, Barron Wilkins's Exclusive Club, Connie's Inn, and scores more, each known for its different style and clientele. One of Bessie Delany's patients owned the famous Small's Paradise, known for waiters who danced the Charleston while balancing full trays of drinks.

The excitement spilled out of the nightclubs and into the community. The less well-to-do would hold "rent parties," where, for a small entrance fee, visitors would drink bathtub gin and dance until dawn, raising money to pay the landlord. Old-timers recall that toward the end of the month in Harlem, handwritten signs for rent parties adorned many public places.

But despite its carefree, high-living image, Harlem had a stable, churchgoing side. There was an old saying that one hundred churches could close their doors in Harlem and there would still have been enough preachers to meet the needs of the people. Political leadership often sprang from the pulpits. The Reverend Adam Clayton Powell and later his son, Adam Clayton Powell Jr., the legendary Congressman, led the powerful Abyssinian Baptist Church, which was the wealthiest Negro Baptist congregation in the world.

Harlem was a magnet for an entire generation of young black Americans with dreams of a better life. By the early 1930s, there were more than 200,000 black people living in Harlem. Among those who made the pilgrimage were nine of the Delany children, who would soon make a niche for themselves in Harlem society.

15

SADIE AND BESSIE

We made our first trip to New York City with our Mama in 1915. We took the train from Raleigh to Norfolk, then took a boat to New York, which cost us eight dollars each. The boat left Norfolk in the afternoon. We slept on cots on the open deck, and woke up just as the boat pulled into New York harbor.

Somebody asked us if we remembered seeing the Statue of Liberty as we pulled into the harbor. Tell you the truth, we didn't care too much about it. The Statue of Liberty was important to white European immigrants. It was a symbol to them. We knew it wasn't meant for us.

On that first visit, we could not get over the size of New York. Papa had been there once, and had tried to describe it, but it was beyond our imagination. The bridges and buildings were on a massive scale compared to anything we had ever seen.

And there were so many different *kinds* of people, from all over the world. In North Carolina, there were white people, Negroes, and Indians. That was it. In New York, there were Irish people, German people, Jewish people, Italian people, and so on. So many different white people! And they ate different foods, and you could smell strange things cooking when you walked by people's apartments in the nice weather when their windows were open. And you'd hear these voices, speaking languages — well, you could only guess what exotic place they were from, and what they were saying.

You could buy anything in New York. We had thought we were so sophisticated, being from Raleigh, where you could get things like fruit from Florida shipped in by train. That was a big deal! But in New York, Raleigh seemed pretty small.

On that first trip we stayed with friends of the family for a few days, then we went home. But we wanted more! So when we returned to Raleigh, we talked to Papa about us moving to New York to attend college. Our brother Harry was already there, working as a Pullman porter, saving money to attend New York University. By then we were grown women, twenty-four and twenty-six years old, and toughened up by our rural teaching years. So when a Presbyterian minister asked Mama, "Aren't y'all afraid to let those girls go up to Harlem-town?" Mama said, "No, I'm not afraid to let my girls go anywhere. We've taught them right from wrong and if they don't do what's right, there's nothing we can do about it."

So we had Mama and Papa's blessing, sort of.

Of the two of us, it was Sadie who made the move first, in 1916, followed by Bessie a year and a half later. Eventually, all of us Delany children, except Lemuel, moved to New York City.

Now, it was awfully hard to find an apartment in Harlem then. There were a lot of colored folks coming to Harlem at the same time, looking for a new life. So looking for an apartment was like a full-time job in itself. You'd have to go from one place to the next, and the super would say, "There's no room now, but come back next month and see." And you'd come back, but somebody had always beat you to the punch.

So, it was common for people to take in boarders. Our brothers were boarding over at the Williamses' house, and we Delany girls boarded with the Scotts. The Scotts were a West Indian family, rather well-to-do. Mr. Scott worked in a white bank, which was absolutely unheard of for a colored man in those days, but he was very light. Like many West Indians, Mrs. Scott was a follower of Marcus Garvey.★ She would drop whatever she was doing and run off to his parades and meetings.

A lot of the West Indian Negroes thought they were better than American Negroes, and the American Negroes thought they were better than

---

★ Marcus Garvey (1887-1940) was the founder of the Universal Negro Improvement Association. He believed that black people in the Americas should recolonize in Africa. While his plan never materialized, Garvey is credited with fostering racial pride. A magnetic leader, Garvey was said to have had a half-million followers.

the West Indian Negroes. One thing about the West Indian Negroes at that time was that the ones who came to Harlem to go to school were a better class than the ones who came to get jobs. There was some silly tension.

Mrs. Scott had taken us in as a favor to Mrs. Russell, who lived across the street and ran a boardinghouse, only it was full. Mrs. Russell had been a pupil of Mama's. But Mr. Scott really didn't want us "boarders" living in his home, and so the whole time we lived at the Scotts we never once ate in the dining room. They made us eat in the kitchen. It wasn't ideal, but it was the best we could do.

Our brother Lucius was the first one of us to get an apartment and he let us all move in with him. So there we were — Sadie, Bessie, Julia, Hubert, and Lucius — living together in a three-room apartment at 2505 Seventh Avenue at the corner of 145th Street. This was in about 1919. Our share of the rent was nine dollars each.

We were packed like sardines in that apartment, and the neighbors across the airshaft complained about us. They were colored people like ourselves. Well, they apparently had the idea these nice-looking colored girls were entertaining these nice-looking colored boys. They thought we were running a fast house! We don't know why it didn't occur to them that we were brothers and sisters, except they must have had unclean minds. So we had a little talk with the super and straightened out the whole mess.

On the ground floor of our building there was a butcher shop owned by Mr. Steinberg, who was a Jewish man. He was very encouraging to all of us Delanys. He would see us come and go to classes, or to our jobs, and he would say good-naturedly, "Now, hurry up! Don't be late!" He was very pleased that we were getting an education.

Poor Lucius! It was his apartment, but his sisters were the boss. Sadie was the oldest, and therefore the head of the household. It worked like this: When a decision had to be made, Sadie had the last word, but Bessie kept everybody in line. Now, Lucius was the best-looking one in the family. He was so good-looking the women would go crazy. And for a while, there was this girl who was flirting with Lucius who just about annoyed us all to death. She would ring the buzzer, and when we'd run down five flights of stairs from our apartment to open the door, there would be no one there. We finally figured it out, and Bessie straightened Lucius right out. She said, "Lucius, our Mama and our Papa trusted us to come live here. We must behave in an adult fashion. We must not let them down!" And Lucius listened. He was a good brother. That girl didn't come around anymore.

Still, it wasn't always easy living with our brothers. They would take our brand-new stockings and wear them on their heads at night, to straighten their hair. Oooh-weee, did that ever make us mad!

The only brother who wouldn't mind us one

bit was Manross, when he'd come to visit. He was stubborn as a mule. He took after Mr. Miliam, our white grandpa. He even looked like him, only he was colored and Mr. Miliam was white as a lily. If you tried to tell Manross what to do, he'd just stare at you.

Manross was in the ROTC at Shaw University in Raleigh, and the next thing we knew, he had gotten swept up into World War I. Funny thing about that war, it happened overseas but it created bloodshed among us here at home. A lot of white people did not think colored men would serve our country with dignity. They thought they'd be cowards. Well, they didn't know Manross!

Like Manross, all the colored veterans came back just as proud as they could be, strutting around Harlem and everywhere else in the country in their uniforms. Manross and his buddies thought they had proved themselves. They thought they would surely come home and be treated like citizens. Manross was very disappointed, because white folks sometimes gave him dirty looks or made nasty remarks when he'd wear his uniform. Manross said, "What more do I have to do to prove I'm an American, too?"

But a lot of white people were mad. They were saying, "Who do these colored boys think they are?" There were riots in Harlem, and lynchings in the South, because white people wanted to put us back in our place.

While this mess was going on, we just worked like dogs, trying to improve ourselves, and counting our blessings that we had the chance. As far as we were concerned, Harlem was as close to Heaven as we were going to find on this Earth.

16

SADIE

Harlem, and all of New York, for that matter, was a happier place then. It was much safer. I used to walk through the parks without any trouble, and you didn't have to worry about somebody shooting at you. Still, it was a meaner place than Raleigh. One day, I was looking out the window at the house where we were boarding when a man stopped and waved to me. So I smiled and waved back. And the landlady said to me, "Sadie Delany, what on earth are you doing? This is not North Carolina!"

You see, in Raleigh, when you'd walk down the street people nodded at each other and said "Good morning" or "Good evening." Men would tip their hat at you and didn't mean anything other than a little sign of respect. In New York, it meant they wanted something else entirely. You were foolish to be friendly to strangers in New York.

Another time, when Bessie and I were new to New York, we went for a long walk one afternoon. We walked out over a bridge, and turned to look at the view of the city. There was no one around but this white man, who looked at us kind of strangely. Then he came to where we were standing and said to us: "What are you two girls doing out here by yourselves?" We were scared to death of this man at first, so we didn't answer. Then he said: "Listen to me, you two girls don't know what you're doing. My wife was robbed here last week. You shouldn't be here. Go on home."

Bessie said to me, "Sadie, this is an omen. We have got to listen to this man. He is a prophet." So, we went home immediately. It was almost as if Papa was still keeping his eye on us.

When I first came to New York, I was so green I don't know how I survived. I was shy, but I was determined. I just kept hearing Papa's voice: "You are college material. And if you don't go, shame on you!"

I set my sights high. I sure didn't pick the easy way when I chose Pratt Institute. Back then, in 1916, they used to say about Pratt: "They'll either make an excellent teacher out of you or flunk you."

One problem was that I was lonely. There were just two of us colored girls in the domestic science division at Pratt Institute when I enrolled, and the other girl dropped out.

I had a difficult time at first, because I really had to scramble in courses like chemistry. At Saint Aug's there were no chemistry labs, so I was weak in that area. That was a problem for a lot of colored students. Often, our early training was not as good as the white students' because colored schools had no money. Then, you had to struggle to keep up if you got into a white college, and white people would label you "dumb."

I remember that I got an A on the chemistry final exam, but then the teacher gave me a C for the course. He said it was because I wouldn't raise my hand and participate in class. He said I was lazy! But I was a little shy, and I found chemistry hard, and I was afraid I'd give the wrong answer. So I kept my mouth shut. I protested the grade, though, because I felt an A on the final exam spoke for itself! They compromised with me and I got a B.

The problem is, you don't always know for sure whether people are being nasty because you're colored, or for some other reason. I remember we had to take swimming at Pratt, and the instructor came along and just shoved my head under water. Now, wasn't that a mean thing to do? Maybe it was because I was colored; I don't know.

Then, for my final semester at Pratt I had to borrow $25 from the school. Papa wouldn't have liked that. Well, I paid that money back as fast as I could. To my surprise, I got a letter from them several years later demanding payment of the $25. I was a little insulted. I was able to prove to them that I had already paid it. And I told them I thought they should have written a nicer letter. They shouldn't have assumed I was a deadbeat! When you're colored, people think you are dishonest.

I'll tell you something else about Pratt. When

I graduated in 1918, it cost $2.50 a year to be a member of the alumni association, or $25 for a life membership. Well, I did what I always do when it comes to money: I thought about it carefully and then figured I should go for the life membership. It would be a good deal over the long run. So I bought that life membership and they've been sorry ever since. If I had paid by the year, by now that would be $187!

Way back then, Pratt was a two-year college. After graduation, I enrolled at Columbia University's Teachers College. I was set on getting a four-year degree.

I was very happy at Columbia. Bessie had a harder time there, when she enrolled in the dental school in 1919. I did not encounter as much prejudice. Maybe it was because I was less noticeable; I was lighter. Or maybe it was because I was quieter. Maybe it was easier to accept a colored woman studying to be a teacher than learning to be a dentist.

One thing they did to me at Columbia, though, is that they tried to get me assigned to a Negro settlement school — the Henry Street Settlement — for my practice teaching, instead of the New York City public schools. Of course, this was because I was colored. Well, I had already *done* practice teaching at the Henry Street Settlement, when I was at Pratt. And I didn't want to do it again. I wanted to do my practice teaching in the New York City public schools, with the other teachers. I didn't fight them over it at Columbia; I just kept

143

reminding them about what I wanted, every chance I got. They gave in, finally.

As much as possible, I kept a low profile at Columbia. Once, when I gave a presentation, the teacher said, "Why, Miss Delany, you act like you've been in the classroom all your life." Well, I had been, growing up at Saint Aug's! But I had sense enough to keep my mouth shut.

I had saved enough money for tuition and rent in New York, but in the summer I'd go home to Raleigh to work to boost up my savings account. When I graduated from Columbia with a bachelor of science in 1920, I actually went back to my old Jeanes Supervisor job. I had this foolish idea I would get paid more, now that I had graduated from Columbia's Teachers College in New York City. I guess I was making about $45 a month, and out of that I had to pay my own expenses. I wasn't militant, like Bessie, but I worked up my nerve and I went to the man in charge and asked — very politely, of course — for more money. And he said, "Why Miss Delany, we can't give you more than we give the white supervisor." And so they wouldn't increase my pay.

Even though my original intention was to graduate from college in New York and return to North Carolina and help my people, I knew I had to return to New York to live. I figured I'd just have to help my people up *there*. I couldn't stand being treated as bad as I was in North Carolina. New York was no piece of cake for a colored person, but it was an improvement over the South, child.

But don't go thinking I don't love the South. I was born there, and I expect to be buried there, right next to my Mama and my Papa. Raleigh will always be home.

17

BESSIE

I had always dreamed I would become a medical doctor, but I ran out of time and money. I was in my late twenties already and I would have needed a few more credits to get into medical school. I was worried that by the time I earned the money and took those classes, I'd be too old.

So I picked up some science courses at Shaw University in Raleigh with the intention of being ready to enroll in a dental degree program in New York. My brother Harry was a dentist, and he was going to see if I could enroll at New York University, where he had graduated. But this was in 1918, and New York University would not take women in its dentistry program.

Instead, I enrolled at Columbia University. This was in the fall of 1919. There were eleven women out of a class of about 170. There were about six colored men. And then there was me. I was the only colored woman!

Columbia was intimidating, but so was everything else. The city was exciting and terrifying at the same time. I couldn't understand why the high-rise buildings didn't fall down, and the subway, well, that about worried me to death! A classmate of mine at Columbia said, "Let's try that old subway." And I said, "I don't think so." And he said, "What, are you afraid?" And I said, "Of course not! If you're willing to try it, so will I!" So we went and everything worked out OK, though once we were on it, I remember whispering to him, "You sure you know how we can get off this thing?"

Most of the students at the dental school were self-assured city folk, and their families were paying their tuition. I never had the luxury of focusing completely on my studies. I always had money on my mind. I needed more, honey! I had saved money from my teaching years in the South, but it wasn't enough. I remember that I always wore an old brown sweater to my classes, because I couldn't even afford a coat. One day, my brother Harry surprised me. He bought me a beautiful coat, with a small fur collar! When I put that coat on, honey, I looked sensational. I looked as good as Mrs. Astor's pet mule. And the first time I wore it to class, the students stood up and applauded. In a way, it was mean, because they were sort of making fun of me. It was like, "Oh, that Bessie Delany finally has something decent to wear." But I didn't care, no, sir!

My brothers were having the same difficulty with money, so they all worked their way through college as Pullman porters, which was one of the few jobs a Negro man could get. Hubert used to joke that he had earned an MBC degree — "master's of baggage carrying."

It was always harder for a Negro to get work than a white person. Even the street merchants in Harlem, in those days, were mostly white. There were certain companies that were nicer to colored people than others. For instance, everybody knew that Nestlé's would hire Negroes, but Hershey's wouldn't. Once I had encountered that, I used to walk through Harlem and scold any Negro eating a Hershey bar. Usually, they would stop eating it but sometimes they thought I was crazy. Well, honey, I do not allow Hershey candy in my home to this day.

As a woman, you couldn't be a Pullman porter, and I refused to work as a maid for white folks. So in the summer, I would go with my little sister Julia, who had come up from Raleigh to study at Juilliard, to look for factory jobs. And you know what? They would want to hire Julia, because she was lighter than me. But we made it clear it was both of us or neither of us, and sometimes we'd get the job.

Once, we had an assembly-line job where they made sewing needles, and our job was to package them in these little batches, so they were ready for sale. Then for a while, we worked as ushers at a movie house. The pay was $12 a week, and we saw all these wonderful movies. My favorite movie star was Bing Crosby. Lord, we had fun. But I was always treated worse than Julia, and it was made clear that it was because I was darker-skinned. Julia was quite light — more like Sadie — and I guess she might even have passed for white if she had tried.

One time, we were waiting on line to get factory work and this white man tried to give me a break. It was always a white guy who was in charge, of course. He said, "Oh, I see. You are Spanish." This was supposed to be my cue to nod my head, since they'd hire you if you were "Spanish." But this made me furious. I said, "No, I am not Spanish. I am an *American Negro!*" I turned and walked out of there and Julia followed me.

Today I know they have this thing called Affirmative Action. I can see why they need it. There are some places where colored folks would *never,* not in a thousand years, get a job. But you know what? I really am philosophically against it. I say: "Let the best person get the job, period." Everybody's better off in the long run.

It was probably a good thing that I was a little older, mature, and so determined or I never would have made it through dental school. I had a few girlfriends, but I never told any of them that I was about ten years older. I never talked about where I came from, my teaching years, or any of that. I was always a big talker, but at dental school I was a private person. There was one girl in particular who used to bug me. She would say, "Bessie, how old are you?" or "Bessie, were you a teacher before you came to dental school?" But I didn't tell her anything.

The reason I was so secretive is that I wanted to be taken seriously. Most of the women were not taken seriously. Truth is, it was just after World War I and a lot of men were still overseas, or killed, so those girls were just looking for husbands. But not me. The boys, well, I stayed away from them. The white boys looked down on me and the colored boys were too busy trying to goose my behind! I had no interest in their shenanigans. I was a good-looking gal, and that always got me in trouble. But I was there to learn!

Before I enrolled in dental school I had a long talk with my Mama. She said, "You must decide whether you want to get married someday, or have a career. Don't go putting all that time and effort into your education and career if you think you want to get married."

It didn't occur to anyone that you could be married *and* have a career. Well, I set my sights on the career. I thought, what does any man really have to offer me? I've already raised half the world, so I don't feel the desire to have babies! And why would I want to give up my freedom and independence to take care of some man? In those days, a man expected you to be in charge of a perfect household, to look after his every need. Honey, I wasn't interested! I wasn't going to be bossed around by some man! So the men at college learned to leave me alone, after a while. There was no foolin' with me! In my yearbook, under the picture, they wrote: "Bessie Delany, the Perfect Lady." And that was the truth.

I studied very hard in dentistry school. My brother Harry — he was called "Hap" once he moved to New York — helped me out. He was a sweet brother. He loaned me some dental instruments, which were very expensive — things like that.

I remember like yesterday the first time our class had to do dissections. This was at the morgue at Bellevue Hospital in New York. The first two years of dental school at that time were identical to medical school, and we all had to do them. Sometimes there weren't enough corpses to go around and the dental students would fight for a head because, well, what we really wanted to examine was the teeth and jaw. And some dental students got stuck with body parts that weren't exactly relevant.

Well, that first day all the girls in the class were just a-squealing and a-screaming and a-carrying on. And I strode in there like I was born to do it. They all said, "Look at that Bessie Delany, why, she sure isn't scared." Truth is, I was a wreck. I had never touched a dead body before!

When we were children, the Webb family, who were farmers at Saint Aug's, had a baby that died, and this little girl at the school named Maggie dared Sadie to touch that baby. People weren't propped up in funeral homes the way they are today. You were wrapped in a shroud and laid out in your own parlor, and that's where this baby was. Afterward, I said to Sadie, "Well, what was it like?" And Sadie said, "Oooh, it was just like touching a piece of marble, hard and cold."

Well, I kept thinking about that poor, marble-like baby while I dissected my first cadaver. We had to fish around and look for these veins and arteries and nerves and things. Yes, it was pretty disgusting but I was a great actress. I was determined to be the best dentist there ever was, and I knew I had to get through this!

I'd dissect a cadaver any day, rather than have to deal with some of those old white professors. Yes, sir! To be fair — oh, it's so hard to be fair — I have to admit that some of them treated me just fine, especially the Dean of Students. He was an old white man, yet he was particularly supportive of me. But one instructor really had it out for me. There was an assignment where he failed me, yet I knew my work was good. One of my white girl friends said, "Bessie, let me turn in your work as if it was mine, and see what grade he gives it."

I'll tell you what happened, honey. She passed with my failed work! That was the kind of thing that could make you crazy, as a Negro. It's no wonder some of us have stopped trying altogether. But as my Papa used to say, "Don't ever give up. Remember, they can segregate you, but they can't control your mind. Your mind's still yours." Ain't it the truth.

Another thing that happened to me at Columbia was that I was accused of stealing. Me, Bessie Delany! Honey, I had never stolen nothin' in my life. This is what happened: There was a white girl who was taking expensive dental instruments. Even my things started disappearing, one by one. It was puzzling. They cost a lot of money, and some of mine belonged to Hap, and I took great pains not to lose them. So none of us could understand where this stuff was going off to.

This girl was a dental student, and we learned later that her boyfriend, also a dental student, had talked her into stealing these tools. He was selling them somewhere in New York. Well, it got to the point where they brought in police detectives. And we were summoned in the hallway where our lockers were, and the police asked me to open my locker, and they searched it.

We were all gathered around, and I saw that this girl — her name was Rose — was standing closest to my locker. When it was opened, behind her back she sort of casually tossed a dental instrument in there. No one saw it but me, and I said in a loud voice, "Rose, what did you toss into my locker?" And the detective and everyone else realized what she had done, and she was caught. She was trying to frame me! And she knew she'd have gotten away with it because it would be easy for everyone to believe that this little darkey was a thief. Now, that just kills me.

Would you believe that Rose and her boyfriend were allowed to finish dental school? They graduated! Honey, if it had been me, I would have been expelled. I would have gone to jail.

I'll tell you something else that annoyed me. When they opened my locker, everybody was surprised at how neat it was. They thought Negroes were dirty, sloppy people, but my locker was perfectly clean and neat, and my one uniform — the only one I could afford — was scrubbed, starched, and ironed. The other girls' lockers were pigsties. And the Dean said, "Look at Miss Delany's locker! It is an example to you all."

You see, when you are colored, everyone is always looking for your faults. If you are going to make it, you have to be entirely honest, clean, brilliant, and so on. Because if you slip up once, the white folks say to each other, "See, what'd I tell you." So you don't have to be as good as white people, you have to be *better or the best.* When Negroes are average, *they fail,* unless they are very, very lucky. Now, if you're average and *white,* honey, you can go far. Just look at Dan Quayle. If that boy was colored he'd be washing dishes somewhere.

There are plenty of white folks who say, "Why haven't Negroes gotten further than they have?" They say about Negroes, "What's wrong with them?" To those white people, I have this to say: *Are you kidding?*

Let me tell you something. Even on my graduation day at Columbia, I ran into prejudice. It was the sixth of June, 1923. There I was, getting my Doctor of Dental Surgery Degree, and I was on top of the world. But you know what? The class selected me as the marshall, and I thought it was an honor. And then I found out — I heard them talking — it was because no one wanted to

154

march beside me in front of their parents. It was a way to get rid of me. The class marshall carried the flag and marched out front, alone.

I suppose I should be grateful to Columbia, that at that time they let in colored people. Well, I'm not. They let me in but they beat me down for being there! I don't know how I got through that place, except when I was young nothing could hold me back. No, sir! I thought I could change the world. It took me a hundred years to figure out I *can't* change the world. I can only change Bessie. And, honey, that ain't easy, either.

18

SADIE

When Papa became bishop in 1918, people were mighty impressed. His accomplishment was so extraordinary, I still wonder how he did it. He put up with a lot to get where he got. One time, not long after Papa was consecrated to the bishopric, he did a service at Christ Church in Raleigh. It was a white, segregated church. Our family attended, and do you know what happened? We had to sit in the balcony, which was built for slaves! And we were not given the privilege of Communion. Ooooh, that makes Bessie mad. At the time, she wanted to make a fuss, but she did not, because she did not want to embarrass Papa.

Somehow, Papa always endured this kind of degradation. He saw the hypocrisy, but he felt that gently, slowly, he was making true progress for himself and his people, and he was at peace with that. I learned a lot from my Papa about coping with institutionalized racism. The way to succeed was simple: You had to be better at what you did than any of your white competition. That was the main thing. But you couldn't be too smug about it, or white folks would feel threatened.

I'll tell you a story. Before I could get my teaching license in New York City, a supervisor named Miss Schermerhorn had come to observe me while I taught a domestic science class. There were three of us student teachers and the assignment was to take a class of young girls and teach them to bake a batch of cookies — how to follow a recipe, and so on. Well, Miss Schermerhorn didn't have time for each of us to go through the whole lesson. So she split up the lesson and I got stuck with the last piece — how to serve and clean up the kitchen efficiently. This was bad because I was dependent on the other girls meeting their deadline ahead of me. I probably got the "cleaning up" part of the assignment because I was colored.

Well, the first girl was a disaster. She panicked, and forgot to halve the recipe. There was enough flour and butter flying around that room to make cookies for the whole world. She also forgot to preheat the ovens. The second girl was supposed to see that the cookies got baked perfectly, but she was so behind because of the first girl that they just made a mess.

Well, then it was my turn. It was clear the first two girls had failed. I thought to myself, Now how am I going to land on my feet here? I just sat those students down and said, "Listen, we have to work together as a team. We only have ten minutes to make the most of this." So we took the rest of the batter and we made those cookies.

And while some of the girls were watching them and taking them out to cool, I had the others lined up to scrub the pans. Then I had them lined up to scrub up themselves.

When my ten minutes were up, we had several dozen perfect cookies, a clean kitchen, and those girls were washed up and ready to go on to their next class. Miss Schermerhorn said to me, "Miss Delany, I don't know how you did that." And she not only passed me, she offered me a substitute teacher's license on the spot. So you see, my way to get ahead was to be better than my white competition. Papa had set a good example for me of how to work within the system.

I got my first teaching job in New York in the fall of 1920. I think I was paid $1,500 for the year. It was at P.S. 119 in Harlem, which was an elementary school, mostly colored. This was a typical assignment for a colored teacher. They most certainly did not want us in schools where the children were white. The parents would object. One way that the principals kept us out was to say they could not hire anyone with a Southern accent because it would be damaging to the children. Well, most of us colored teachers at the time had Southern accents. So it was just a way of keeping us out.

When my Southern accent was considered a problem, I found a way around that. I signed up with a speech coach — a woman in Manhattan. She was a white woman, a lovely woman. I don't think she had too many colored clients. I remember that when I would go to her apartment for the lessons, the doorman made me take the freight elevator. I didn't make a fuss because I wanted those speech lessons.

You had to decide: Am I going to change the world, or am I going to change me? Or maybe change the world a little bit, just by changing me? If I can get ahead, doesn't that help my people?

I was very ambitious. Much of the time that I taught at P.S. 119 I made money on the side by baking cakes and selling them for a nickel a slice to the teachers at school. I would make a cake and cut it into twenty slices, and make a dollar. The ingredients didn't cost me anywhere near that much to buy, so I made a neat profit. Another thing I would do is make lollipops at home and sell them in the school cafeteria for a penny each. Sometimes I'd make lemon; other times I'd make cinnamon, or something else. You might think that making lollipops and cakes is an awful slow way to get money, but I liked doing it. Besides, you'd be surprised at how it adds up — a penny here, a nickel there — after a few years. I never let a nickel get by me, that's what Bessie always says. Why, for several years during the 1920s I even made good money!

You see, Miss Larson, the principal at P.S. 119, got this idea that her boyfriend could peddle my candy. He had trouble holding onto a job and she was looking for something for him to do. So I rented a loft at 121st Street, in the business district. We called the candy "Delany's Delights" and had tins made up with that name. The candy was hand-dipped chocolate fondant and we had three sizes: a half pound, a pound, and two pounds. We charged two dollars per pound and we just sold that stuff all over New York, even at Abraham & Straus, the department store! I made it and he sold it.

Eventually, I gave up the candy business. The Depression came along and people had no money for chocolate fondant, that's for sure. Also, I had begun teaching at a high school, and it was a more demanding schedule than elementary school.

I had wanted to teach at a high school because it was considered a promotion, and it paid better. But I had to be a little clever — Bessie would say sneaky — to find ways to get around these brick walls they set up for colored folks. So I asked around quietly for some advice. A friend of my brother Hubert's who worked for the Board of Education suggested a plan, which I followed.

This is what I did: I applied for a high school position, and when I reached the top of the seniority list after three years, I received a letter in the mail saying they wished to meet with me in person. At the appointment, they would have seen I was colored and found some excuse to bounce me down the list. So I skipped the appointment and sent them a letter, acting like there was a mix-up. Then I just showed up on the first day of classes. It was risky, but I knew what a bureaucracy it was, and that in a bureaucracy it's easier to keep people out than to push them back down.

Child, when I showed up that day — at Theodore Roosevelt High School, a white high school — they just about died when they saw me. A colored woman! But my name was on the list to teach there, and it was too late for them to send me someplace else. The plan had worked! Once I was in, they couldn't figure out how to get rid of me.

So I became the first colored teacher in the New York City system to teach domestic science on the high school level. I spent the rest of my career teaching at excellent high schools! Between 1930 and 1960, when I retired, I taught at Theodore Roosevelt High School, which is on Fordham Road in the Bronx, then at Girls' High School in Brooklyn, and finally at Evander Childs High School, which is on Gun Hill Road in the Bronx.

Plus, I got a night job — at Washington Irving High School in lower Manhattan — teaching adults who had dropped out of school. This was something I really wanted to do. The way I got the job was that the girl who had it before me complained a lot, was late a lot, and would ask me to substitute for her. Eventually, they just hired me instead of her! But that's the way you get ahead, child. Even if you're colored, if you're good enough, you'll get the job. As long as they *need* you, you've got that job.

Meanwhile, I was studying for my master's degree in education at Columbia, which I completed in 1925. I was a busy gal, but I was happy being busy. My classes were usually very demanding because as a colored teacher, I always got the meanest kids. Except once. That was the year they had me mixed up with a white woman whose name also was Delany. It was kind of funny. She was just furious, because she got all these tough girls, and I got the easy ones — college-bound and motivated. Tell you the truth, I did not mind the tough kids. I loved them all.

It was lonely being about the only colored teacher around. Sometimes the white teachers were friendly, but you couldn't count on any of them being your real friends. There was one woman I was friendly with, and we decided to meet on a Saturday and go swimming at a public pool in the Bronx. I remember that when she saw me in my bathing suit, she looked at my legs and said, "Why, Sarah, you are very white!" And I said, "So what?" I guess she was surprised that I didn't try to pass for white.

Personally, I never had any desire to be white. I am absolutely comfortable with who I am. I used to laugh at how both races seem to hate their hair. All these Negro ladies would run out and get their hair *straightened,* and all these white ladies would run out and get their hair *curled.* My hair was in-between, with a little kink in it, just enough to give it body. I had no desire to change it. I had no desire to change me. I guess I owe that to my Mama and Papa.

This same teacher who seemed to wonder why I didn't just try to "pass" turned out to be a fair-weather friend. Once, she and I had planned to go swimming, and she said to wait under the clock at noon, and so I did. But coincidentally, some other white girls she knew showed up right when she arrived. So she just snubbed me. She didn't want them to know we were friends, so she left me standing there and walked on past, with them. She was so obvious that there really wasn't anything to do but laugh it off and forget about it.

I remained on friendly terms with that woman. Bessie says, "I wouldn't have had nothing more to do with her this side of Glory!" This is the kind of thing that drives Bessie wild. Bessie would have given her a piece of her mind. Sure, it annoyed me. But I didn't let it ruin my day. Life is short, and it's up to you to make it sweet.

19

BESSIE

I was known in the Negro community as "Dr. Bessie" to distinguish me from my brother Hap, who was known as "Dr. Delany." There was a time, in the 1920s, '30s, and '40s in Harlem when just about every living soul knew of Dr. Bessie. My patients would go on vacation and send post-cards addressed only to "Dr. Bessie, New York City" and I would get those cards.

In those days, folks were probably more attached to their dentists than today. They saw more of their dentists because their teeth were worse, generally. Today there's fluoride in the water, and better toothbrushes and floss, plus people are better educated about oral hygiene than they used to be.

When we were children, we had no toothbrushes. We would take little switches from a peach tree and rub them on our teeth. Actually, it did a pretty good job. Sadie and I still brush our teeth with equal parts of baking soda and salt, mixed into a paste with a little water in the palm of your hand. And once a week, we wash our teeth with our homemade soap. Hap used to say there was nothing that made for a gleaming smile more than homemade soap! Sounds funny, but it's true.

Hap was four years younger than me but he was already finishing school and starting his practice by the time I got to dental school. When I graduated, he invited me to share an office with him and another dentist, Dr. Chester Booth, at 2305 Seventh Avenue — that's the corner of Seventh Avenue and 135th Street. We were on the second floor, above the Corn Exchange Bank, which later became the Chemical Bank.

This was the center of Harlem! From the office window you could see everything that was going on. Harlem was like a beehive, with people running every which way, going to work, school, or to entertainment. It was a positive place.

There were some colorful folks, like this peculiar man that people called the Barefoot Prophet. In actuality, I suppose he was a hobo, but he looked like Jesus Christ. He had long hair, and wore long, flowing robes, and he'd march around barefoot in Harlem. And there was this fella named Father Divine. He was a Negro minister whose background was a mystery. People said he could do supernatural things, like perform miracles and heal the sick. At his church, which was across from St. Martin's Church at 122nd Street and Lenox Avenue, they had a great big dining hall, where they fed all the hungry in Harlem. At that time, Father Divine had a huge following. His followers thought he was God. Now, those are the fellas you have to watch out for, the ones who think they are God. Look out!

Hap and I loved having our offices in the middle of everything. After a while, we moved next door — to 2303 Seventh Avenue — where we shared a suite of offices with our brother Lucius, who was an attorney, along with a Negro real estate agent, and Dr. MacDonald, a Negro dentist from Trinidad who had gone to Saint Aug's. We had our own X-ray lab, a technician, and two mechanics who were hired by me and Hap to make dentures and bridges. I was the only woman among the bunch of us, and I ran the show. On the day the rent was due, I'd say, "OK, fellas, pay up!" Somehow, among all those men, I ended up being the boss.

In those days, many people simply would not go to a woman dentist. There were so very few women dentists at all, never mind colored women dentists. Why, I was only the second Negro woman licensed to practice in New York. I was also only the second Negro woman to get a dental license in North Carolina. (I got my license there, thinking I might go back someday.)

It was bad enough to be discriminated against by white people because I was colored. But then, my own people would discriminate against me because I was a woman! Two times I remember that men patients of mine insisted that Hap come and pull their teeth. I remember one man said to me, "Can you pull teeth with those little hands?"

166

and I said, "Do you really want to find out?" It made me mad. I could take those forceps and pull just as hard as any man. That sexism was a nasty thing to deal with. But once a person had been my patient, they'd always come back. The word got out: That colored woman dentist has a gentle touch.

Every colored person in New York knew that I would take any patient, no matter how sick. We had the same concerns then about contagious diseases as there are today about this new disease, AIDS. It was a human reaction that dentists had; we were afraid of getting infectious diseases from our patients. It was human, but it wasn't professional.

Back in dental school, I treated a little white girl with syphilis who came to the school clinic. I imagine she was born with it. It just about broke my heart. She was sitting in the hallway alone, crying, and my classmates just about broke their legs trying to run away from her. Not one of them would touch her, so I volunteered. I said to them, "What do you think it's going to be like in the real world, when we graduate? Are you just going to run away from people who need your help?"

In those days, we did not wear gloves. But I always took care of my hands. I was careful to avoid getting cuts and I kept my nails very short. Now, I am almost embarrassed when I go to the dentist — embarrassed for my profession, I mean. They come at you with these masks and gowns; they look like they're from outer space. When I

167

went to school, you became a doctor or dentist in order to help people. Society respected you for taking risks.

Even then, of course, there were those who wanted society's respect but did not earn that esteem. For instance, there were many dentists in my day who would not take colored patients. That was why it was so important that there were colored dentists! One time, after graduation, a white classmate of mine from Columbia called me up and said he was sending over a patient. At first, I thought he was doing me a favor, but then he mentioned that it was his maid. And I realized he didn't want to work on her mouth because she was colored. So I said to him, "You are not a doctor of dentistry! You are a doctor of segregation!" I yelled at him so loud he hung up. Well, his maid came over and of course I helped her. But I never spoke to him again.

And there were those who only wanted the money. Some dentists would even do poor quality work, just to make the patient uncomfortable so that he'd have to come back. It would never have occurred to me to do that. No, sir! When I started my practice in 1923, I charged two dollars for a cleaning, two dollars for an extraction, five dollars for a silver filling, and ten dollars for a gold filling. When I retired in 1950, I was still charging the same rate. I never raised my rates because I was getting by OK. I was always very proud of my work, and that was enough for me.

I never turned anyone away because they

couldn't pay me. Back when I was a young dentist, a child could not enroll in New York City public schools without a dental exam. This was tricky for a lot of poor, colored parents because they couldn't afford it. Honey, I must have done thousands of those dental exams without charge. But it was rare that someone outright stole my services. One time comes to mind, when I worked on a man's teeth, and he said he had to run down the street to do something and would be right back, and he never came back. So I never got paid. But usually, people would find a way to pay me, or they paid me eventually.

Not all the patients were poor. Hap and I had separate practices, and he had a large number of famous people, such as Walter White[*] of the NAACP and entertainers like Bojangles Robinson and Alberta Hunter, who was one of the nicest women I ever knew. But some of Hap's jazz friends were annoying because they always wanted to use the phone. I still remember the number. It was the most well-used phone in Harlem! Once, the bill was $100 and I nearly fainted dead on the floor. That was a lot of money in those days and those jazz folks never did chip in to pay us back, even though they had more cash than anybody. So you know what I did? I went and had a pay phone put in.

[*] Walter White (1893–1955) was the executive secretary of the National Association for the Advancement of Colored People from 1931 to 1955. Born in Atlanta of mixed black and white parentage, White used his light complexion to investigate and write exposés about lynchings and race riots.

I had a few famous patients of my own, including Ed Small, the nightclub owner, and Dr. Louis T. Wright[1] — I was also his patient — and Dr. Wright's family. I also took care of James Weldon Johnson,[2] and once he gave me a signed copy of a book of poetry he had just published, and there were only five hundred copies printed. My patients were as nice to me as I was to them.

But there were people who couldn't stand the very idea of a colored woman being a dentist, and they weren't shy about letting me know. Once, about 1925, I went to a medical conference at the Hotel Pennsylvania in Manhattan. I remember I had borrowed Sadie's horsehair turban, and I thought I looked very attractive, very professional. I went up to the front desk and identified myself as a dentist who was to attend the meeting, and this white fella looked at me like I was some little monkey that had just fallen out of a tree and landed in his soup and ruined his day. I asked him for directions to my meeting. Yes, he gave me directions — to the *men's toilet*.

When I found myself standing in front of the men's room instead of the conference room, I was

[1] Dr. Louis T. Wright (1891–1952) was a New York surgeon and civil rights leader who served as chairman of the board of the NAACP from 1935 to 1952. He often combined his two passions — medicine and civil rights — by promoting better health care for black Americans.
[2] James Weldon Johnson (1871–1938) was the first executive secretary of the NAACP,was well as a diplomat, poet, and anthologist of black American literature. With his brother, John Rosamond Johnson, a composer, he wrote "Lift Every Voice and Sing," which is often called the Negro national anthem.

so filled with rage that I couldn't move. Fortunately, one of my former classmates — he happened to be white — saved me from total humiliation. He saw me standing there and said, "Bessie Delany, what in the world are you doing *here?*" And he just took my arm and escorted me to the conference like I was the queen of England.

That day was one of the lowest points of my life, but I didn't have time to dwell on it. I often worked about fifteen hours a day. The only time I ever closed my office early was when one of my patients died, because I would go to the funeral. Wednesday was supposed to be my day off, but often I spent it covering for Hap while he and Dr. Chester Booth ran the Harlem Dental Clinic, which they founded with the help of the Urban League.

During the week, I had no free time for myself. I had to get up at daybreak and go to the office and clean and disinfect it, since I was always too exhausted at the end of the day to sterilize things properly, and I couldn't afford a cleaning lady. To save money, I walked ten blocks to work rather than ride the trolley or the subway, which cost five cents. I'd walk home again after cleaning the office, then bathe, and walk back to the office in time to open up at nine o'clock, looking fresh out of a bandbox.

For a while, I had a beau who would drive me to work. He was the brother of a dentist I knew. One day, I went on a date with this man and we drove to the Palisades in New Jersey. We were parked, looking over the edge of these cliffs, when this fella got crazy on me. He said: "I could just hit the gas, and we'd go right over the edge and we'd both be dead. We would both *die*."

And I thought, Oh, Bessie Delany, you have got yourself in a fine mess. But I just said, "Now, what would you want to do that for?" as calmly as possible, like it was a joke. But it wasn't a joke. This fella was nuts.

Finally, after threatening me for a while longer, he quieted down and drove me home. But would you believe the next morning that fella was parked at the curb, as if nothing had happened, ready to give me a ride to work? I felt like yelling at him, "You are crazy!" but for once in my life, I kept my mouth shut and just said, "No, thanks, I'd rather walk" in a friendly way. Still, that fella followed me to my office every day for weeks.

I know it sounds like I *lived* at my office, but I did make room in my life for relaxation. If I hadn't, I wouldn't have lived this long! Saturday was often a day for fun, and sometimes I'd go shopping with Sadie, or on a picnic with a beau. Occasionally, I'd be real naughty and go to the horse races on Long Island. I would bet a little money, say, five dollars. But I always won! So did Sadie. Our men friends would ask, "How do y'all always know which horse to pick?" Well, we studied the horses carefully before the race, and since we grew up around animals, we knew which ones were winners. And of course, I was a little psychic about these things.

I guess our most favorite pastime of all was baseball. We weren't too far away from the team which became the Yankees, but they were slow to integrate so we weren't interested in them. Sadie and I loved Walter Johnson, a pitcher for the Washington team. If he was pitching in New York, we were there! But we were really Giants fans. The day I heard they were moving out to San Francisco, well, I was beside myself with sorrow. I said, "How can they do this to me?" I was a-carrying on like somebody had up and died.

Another thing we used to do was go to the Old Bronx Opera house, where they used to preview Broadway plays. You could go there real cheap and see the best musicals New York had to offer. It only cost fifty cents if you sat in the balcony.

I remember being at the Old Bronx Opera house once with Papa, who must have come up from Raleigh with Mama to see us. This must have been about 1925. Well, Papa was nervous because it was Lent and he didn't think he should be at the Old Bronx Opera house. He said, "What if someone sees me?" Papa always did care about appearances. But I think it was because he had to; it was part of getting ahead. White people were watching you all the time, just waiting for you to make a mistake. So we not only *lived* a clean life, we wanted to be sure people *knew* that we did.

This is a burden that white people do not have, I think. It always seemed to me that white people were judged as individuals. But if a Negro did something stupid or wrong, it was held against *all* of us. Negroes were always representing the whole race.

All I ever wanted in my life was to be treated as an individual. I have succeeded, to some extent. At least I'm sure that in the Lord's eyes, I am an individual. I am not a "colored" person, or a "Negro" person, in God's eyes. I am just me! The Lord won't hold it against me that I'm colored because He made me that way! He thinks I am beautiful! And so do I, even with all my wrinkles! I am beautiful!

20

SADIE

One thing that happened to a lot of colored folks when they moved to Harlem was that they got a little too big for their britches. They thought they'd got to be important by living in Harlem. When they'd go back to visit their folks in the South, the men acted like dudes, and the women acted like they thought they were the Queen of Ethiopia.

Well, I guess we thought we were a little special, too, but Mama and Papa kept us in line. The first time I went home, I said "darn" in front of my Mama and she gave me a piece of her mind. She said, "Is that what you've learned, up there in New York? You've learned how to swear?" She shamed me good. I never swore again.

Well, we heard a few racy words in Harlem, child. Harlem was the playground for the rich. You couldn't help but run into flashy Negroes and high-living white folks. From 1920 to 1933, Prohibition was going on, and you couldn't drink legally, but that didn't stop anybody.

Still, it is a white stereotype that everybody in Harlem did nothing but drink and play around and go to nightclubs. The poorest Negroes were busy scratching out a living working for white folks as servants. Those folks probably never saw the inside of a nightclub, unless they were mopping the floor.

Being good girls, Bessie and I did not venture too far into the jazz scene. After all, we were Bishop Delany's daughters. We didn't want to have anything to do with smooth-talking men and their fast women. If we went to a nightclub, it was always with a proper escort. Usually, we went to places like Ed Small's. Once, Bessie went to the Cotton Club, which was hard to do because they had colored performers but it was a white folks' club. Bessie got in, because she had a beau who worked there.

Our brother Hubert became friendly with many famous entertainers. Eventually, he bought a weekend house upstate and people like Cab Calloway used to go up there to visit. Once, I remember Bessie and I were to go up with Cab Calloway in his car, and Hubert was annoyed because we had all this junk we wanted to bring. Hubert said, "Y'all came up here for the weekend with all that stuff in Cab's car?" I guess we did look kind of like we were about to move in.

Over the years, through friends or through Hubert, we met entertainers like Ethel Waters, Bert Williams, Fletcher Henderson, Duke Ellington, and Lena Horne. We were acquainted with these people, but our circle of close friends was the professional class. For example, one of the frequent guests at our home was Mr. William Kelly, the editor of the *Amsterdam News*, which was a very influential Negro newspaper that is still published in New York today.

Mr. Kelly never passed up an invitation for our cooking. He used to say he felt right at home, except for one thing. He said he never saw anything like the way we Delanys always cleaned our plates. We used to laugh and tell him, "If you'd grown up in a family of ten children that had no money, you'd be in the habit of cleaning your plate, too."

We took great pride in preparing and serving meals for company, and while we didn't have the best china, you'd be surprised what you can do with fresh flowers and pressed linens. We had people over for dinner so often that for years, we kept a journal of what we had served to whom, and when, so that we wouldn't accidentally cook the same thing twice in a row for a guest.

The whole time in Harlem, we lived the same way that we did in Raleigh. We didn't change our values or behavior one bit. Every Sunday was the Lord's day, and you could find us, sure as daylight, at Saint Martin's Episcopal Church.

Knowing that Mama and Papa were counting on us to behave like ladies put the pressure on us to be good. We were very proud of the Delany name, and because of our self-discipline it came to mean in Harlem what it had meant in North

Carolina — that is, it stood for integrity.

We all relied on each other. Throughout the years we lived in Harlem, from World War I until Bessie and I moved to the Bronx after World War II, all of the brothers and sisters saw each other at least once a day. Most often, this was at the dental office. Julia would come by and help with the bookkeeping, and Sam would pop in just to say hello. It was like a revolving door of Delanys.

We even continued to live together. Around 1926 we all chipped in money and Hap took out a mortgage for some cooperatives at 219 West 121st Street. Bessie and I, along with our sisters Julia and Laura, lived in one apartment on the second floor. Our brother Sam lived next door, and our brother Hap and his family lived upstairs.

These were long, narrow apartments, like railroad flats. On holidays, there wasn't room for a sit-down dinner for the whole family, so our younger brothers and sisters would have dinner in their own apartments and come by our place later. At Easter we'd always have a big dish of dyed eggs and the biggest ham we could afford. At Christmas, we'd serve coffee, fruit, and waffles with whipped cream all day long, until no one could eat any more. One Christmas, Hap said he was going to come by and fix us some eggnog. I said, "Come on over, but don't bother with the eggnog, 'cause I hate the stuff." I remembered when Papa gave me a little when Mama had her babies, way back when. Only, Papa gave me eggnog without any liquor in it, of course. Hap laughed at me and said, "Girl, you ain't never had no real eggnog." So he came over and made the real thing — with liquor — and, yes, it was mighty good.

I was a woman in age, but a child in experience. Here Bessie and I were, over thirty years old, living in Harlem in its heyday. And for the first time in our lives, we had *spending money*. We were very stingy with it because Mama and Papa had taught us how to save and how to spend carefully. But they didn't prepare us for folks who wanted to take our money *away*. I don't want to give the impression that the men were all con artists — why, there were lots of nice men. But in Harlem, it seemed like someone was always trying to borrow money from us, and we didn't know how to say no.

One time, I cosigned a loan for a man I didn't know well and I got stuck paying it. It had just never occurred to me that anyone would do that to me. But there I was, owing $700. Well, that was about half of my year's salary! The bank wanted me to pay $70 a month, and I had to explain to them that I could only pay $12.50 per month. It was the best I could do.

Bessie and I became smarter about money. One time, we came up with this idea that we were going to invest five dollars each in the stock market. Women weren't supposed to dabble in the stock market, so everyone laughed at us, but one of Bessie's dental patients said to her, "Buy stock in something called the Creole Petroleum Company." He was a servant at the house of a rich white man who worked on Wall Street. This rich white man would talk openly like the Negro servants were deaf or stupid. Only, this patient of Bessie's was listening to every word, and writing it down!

So, we bought two and a half shares each, and it did pretty well over the years. Then the Creole Petroleum Company was bought by Exxon, and Exxon wanted our puny old shares. They bullied us to sell until finally we gave in. But Bessie said to me at the time, "Sadie, those folks at Exxon are mean, running roughshod over us like this! They are in for some big trouble, someday!"

That's why Bessie and I weren't the least bit surprised when Exxon went and spilled all that oil up in Alaska and everybody in the whole world was just disgusted with them. Bessie said to me, "See. I told you so."

21

BESSIE

White people used to come up to Harlem looking for a good time. They would come up to "nigger town" looking for fun at places like the Cotton Club, where they catered to white folks.

I used to walk home along Seventh Avenue, late at night, after I had closed my office. A lot of my patients were poor and worked during the day, so often it was midnight or one o'clock in the morning by the time I was done. Usually, I managed to avoid the folks who were out rabble-rousing and carrying on, but one night, I was walking past the Hotel Theresa when some drunk white man started harassing me. I guess he thought he was up in nigger town and here was this nigger woman by herself, and maybe he'd found himself something interesting to do.

He grabbed my arm and started slobbering all over me and saying stupid, woozy things that white men say when they've been boozing it up. I said to him, "Get out of my way, fool!" And he stopped short. He let go of my arm. He couldn't believe his ears. And I said, "You are drunk, and you had better let me go or I will get a police officer and he'll throw you in jail!" I knew the precinct house was just around the corner. I had no idea if a police officer would bother to help a Negro woman under the circumstances, but I guess I sounded confident. That white man backed off. He could see I meant business! Yes, he had picked on the wrong woman.

It didn't matter to that white fella — and I doubt it would have mattered to the police — that I was a doctor of dentistry and a good citizen of Harlem. There was little respect from white people, no matter how accomplished you were. It was like you were invisible. It was so strange to be so respected among Negroes, but to white people you were just some little pickaninny.

By the mid-'20s my office had become a meeting place for Negro activists in Harlem, including E. Franklin Frazier.* I met Frazier while we were both at Columbia. Frazier later married my sister-in-law's sister (Lemuel's wife's sister). I suppose I could have married him, but as I've said, I was not interested in marriage, so Frazier and I remained lifelong friends.

One time, I encouraged a friend of Frazier's named Albert Robinson to fight back over a prob-

---

* E. Franklin Frazier (1894–1962) was a sociologist noted for his ground-breaking studies on the Negro family and race relations. He was educated at Columbia University and the University of Chicago, and was a professor of sociology at Fisk University and later head of the sociology department at Howard University.

lem he was encountering in a sociology class at Columbia. He was a graduate student. There was this white professor who told the class that Negroes were inferior to white people, and he demonstrated this with IQ tests taken by children of different races. Robinson, who was colored but looked white, was just incensed. I suggested that he borrow two of Hap's little children to prove that professor wrong. So, this is what happened: Robinson brought these two little Delanys to the class and challenged the professor to prove they were stupid. And the professor said, fine, let them take the IQ test. And you know what? Those two little Delanys scored much higher than the white children.

Frazier and Robinson were real big on staging sit-ins at lunch counters of white restaurants in Harlem that wouldn't serve colored people. But that was not my style of activism at all. I was afraid some nasty white folks would spit in my food in the back, then serve it to me. I didn't want their germs, no, sir. You can yell at me, call me names, hit me, but keep your germs to yourself!

The whites resented the Negroes taking over Harlem, but eventually all of them had to serve Negroes — including at those white-owned restaurants — or go out of business, because after a while there was nobody left but Negroes. White folks had run out of Harlem like fleas from a dead dog.

One time, I got tired of listening to Frazier and his friends planning another sit-in. This was in about 1925. They had just re-released the film

Birth of a Nation, which was a very mean-spirited film which degraded Negroes. It was showing at the Capitol Theater in Manhattan.

So I said to Frazier, "How can y'all sit around here planning those silly sit-ins when they're showing *Birth of a Nation* at the Capitol? I don't know about you, but I'm going down there tonight and protest. And if you don't join me, well, shame on you!"

Well, I guess I inspired them. But what happened is kind of funny, at least to me. Hap had a patient with an emergency and I stayed to help, so we were late. Well, we got there just in time to see the cops throwing poor Frazier and Robinson, along with W. E. B. Du Bois* and Walter White, and a bunch of other protesters, into the police wagon.

The next day, those boys chewed me out good! They came to my office and said, "You convinced us to protest and then you didn't show up! You have a lot of nerve!" And I said, "Well, Hap and I did show up, it's just that y'all were too busy getting yourselves arrested to notice." They didn't think it was too funny.

It was around this time — about 1925 — that I had my one, personal encounter with the Ku Klux Klan. I was on a Sunday outing with Dean,

* Dr. W.E.B. Du Bois (1868–1963) was an intellectual leader of black Americans. He founded the Niagara Movement in 1905, which evolved into the National Association for the Advancement of Colored People by 1910, and edited its publication, *The Crisis*, from 1910 to 1934.

184

my boyfriend at the time, coming back from the beach and heading to his house in Sag Harbor. He was a Negro dentist, a good friend. Well, we came around the corner of this two-lane road, and there were about twenty men dressed in white robes, hoods and all, stopping cars and searching. You could see that they were making colored people get out of their cars!

Well, my eyes about popped out of my head. I said, "Aren't you going to stop?" But my friend never answered me. He stepped on the gas and drove right around them, up an embankment and everything, and next thing I knew we had just zoomed around them. I said, "Lord have mercy, Dean, what are you doing? They'll come after us." Well, Dean's car was a Cadillac and it had a very powerful engine and I believe we simply outran them. Dean drove like a madman all the way back to Sag Harbor.

You should have seen the look on Mama's face when I told her that night what had happened. Here, all those years in the South they had managed to keep us Delany children out of the hands of the KKK and they'd almost got their hands on me — on *Long Island.*

That incident made me become even more of an activist. Honey, all you had to say was the word "protest" and I was there! I marched in more protests in New York City than I care to remember. It's a wonder I didn't wear out my feet.

One time, I participated in a protest march for Negro rights that went from Harlem down to

Fifty-ninth Street. When I ran home from my office to change my clothes, I couldn't find any clean stockings in my drawer. So I did something we never, ever did in our family: I helped myself to a pair of Sadie's stockings, *without asking*. During the march, I wore a hole in Sadie's stockings, and when I got back later I explained what happened and she let it go, on the condition that I replace those stockings with a new pair. But I just realized, after all this time, that I never did buy her a new pair. She never said a word about it, all this time. She is really a very sweet sister.

Sadie never did like marches and protests. She didn't like confrontations. So I told Sadie, "Well, you gave *something* for the cause after all. Your stockings!"

There were a lot of colored people like Sadie. Really, there were the two extremes. On the one hand you had Booker T. Washington, a smoother of the waters, not a radical. Mr. Washington's goals were modest for his race: He wanted you to be literate, to own your forty acres and a mule. Sadie was more like Booker T. Washington.

And on the other hand, you had W.E.B. Du Bois, a militant. I can still see his face: He was a brown-skinned, good-looking man with a mustache, and very intelligent-looking eyes. Dr. Du Bois was the editor of *The Crisis* and was always speaking out against one thing or another, especially about lynchings in the South. Many people thought his approach was too fast, too threatening to white people and therefore dangerous for Negroes. Papa used to say about Dr. Du Bois: "We need leaders like him, he is good for our people. But we can't all be like him." I guess he felt there would be too much blood shed.

Now, Dr. Du Bois knew my Papa because at that time, there were very, very few educated, prominent Negroes. Also, Dr. Du Bois always stayed with my brother Lemuel and his wife when he visited Raleigh. Papa was not aggressive enough by Dr. Du Bois's standards. He thought my Papa was a "handkerchief head" type of Negro — the bowing and stooping kind of field-hand nigger who would let white people push him around. This was not fair, because my Papa had a lot of dignity.

Still, I believed in Dr. Du Bois's approach: I would have given life or limb to the cause. I wanted justice for my people, or a least a better life, a fair shake! Sometimes, colored women were not welcome in the movement, though. You got the message that some of the colored *men* thought the colored *women* should not be involved. Too bad, I was there whether they liked it or not! You couldn't keep me at home.

I was torn between two issues — colored, and women's rights. But it seemed to me that no matter how much I had to put up with as a woman, the bigger problem was being colored. People looked at me and the first thing they saw was *Negro,* not *woman.* So racial equality, as a cause, won in my heart.

But one of the happiest days of my life was back

in 1920, when women got the right to vote. Sadie and I registered to vote immediately and we have never missed a chance to vote since. Now, where we vote, the people at the polls have come to know us. They say, "Here come the Delany sisters. We knew you'd get here, one way or another!"

Negroes, more than anyone, need to make sure they vote, to make themselves heard in the system. We've come a long, long way in a short, short time since slavery days, and there ain't no use in quitting now. It's true that you can't change the world with your one vote, but if you don't vote, you don't have the right to complain. And honey, I surely do not want to give up my right to complain, no, sir!

22

SADIE

People think of the 1920s as the good old days, but of course there were many of the same problems we have now — except then, we didn't have this widespread drug problem, or this thing called AIDS. Still, there was terrible poverty, even in our own family, mostly among our relatives down South.

Bessie and I tried to help them, as much as we could. It was our little project. A lot of those folks did not have refrigeration and we worried they would get sick. So one of the things we did was to buy iceboxes for some of our relatives, especially Mama's folks in Virginia. I think those folks thought we were rich, Bessie and me. But nothing could be further from the truth. All the time we were buying new iceboxes for those folks, we had a broken-down old icebox ourselves.

Among my students in New York City there were plenty of children, white and colored, who had problems. There was one girl who comes to mind from P.S. 119. All the girls made fun of her because she had this mark, like a dark ring, around her neck. Well, it was obvious to me that it was just plain old *dirt!* When there were no other children around I asked her about it, and she said, "My mama says it's a birthmark."

So I said, "Child, I don't think it is. Would you like me to try and fix it?" So she stayed after school and I took her into the girls' room and took a towel and cleaned her neck. Soap and water didn't get it off, so I rubbed cold cream in it, and I rubbed and rubbed until I got it all off. The next day, she came in and said, "Miss Delany, my mama said to thank you so much for cleaning up my neck."

Now, I think that's kind of funny. Imagine not knowing that your child's neck is dirty. Well, there are a lot of people who weren't raised properly themselves, so how can they teach their children right? Sometimes it's neglect, sometimes it's just ignorance. And what people don't know will really hold them back. This is especially true of colored children once they try to succeed among white people in the job market. Being presentable and having good manners — don't underestimate the importance of this, especially if you're colored. It's amazing how many people don't know the basics about simple hand-washing, how to iron a shirt properly, things like that.

That's why you need home economics. Back in the twenties it was called "domestic science." It was nutrition, cooking and canning, sewing, hygiene — anything you can think of that makes a home a proper, healthy environment. Of course, home economics was for girls. Before I retired in 1960, I did have a few boys in my classes. I think it's good for boys to take it, especially now that men are expected to do more around the house.

It was domestic science that brought me the greatest accomplishment of my life: saving Cousin Daisy from dying. Cousin Daisy was Mama's cousin in Virginia. She was a granddaughter of Aunt Pat — the one who had her baby by the side of the road. Well, one day we got a letter that Cousin Daisy was sick. The white doctor in Danville said she had pellagra, and there was nothing could be done. Although she was still a fairly young woman, she was going to die.

Pellagra was a disease that you got from not eating enough vegetables and fresh fruit. First your hair would fall out; then you'd get weak and not be able to walk, and eventually — it might take several years — you had one foot in the grave.

Well, back then, people were just beginning to understand the importance of vitamins and minerals. As a teacher of domestic science, I kept up-to-date on the new developments in nutrition. One day, I saw in the newspaper that Dr. Carlton Fredericks, a scientist who worked with the man who had discovered Vitamin B_{12}, was going to be visiting New York City. So I invited him to my school to speak at an assembly.

After his talk, I took him aside and told him all about Cousin Daisy down in Virginia. I said, "Please, can you help me?" And he told me exactly what to do. So I went and bought these liquid vitamins at a store in New York. You couldn't buy them in Virginia, and I realized that Cousin Daisy and her husband, who was a farmer, would not be able to afford them. I shipped those vitamins to Daisy, along with a schedule for taking them. I also drew up menu plans for her of what I thought she should eat. She was eating too much fatback and cornbread, things like that.

Well, that old white doctor in Danville was wrong. There *was* something could be done for Cousin Daisy. With those vitamins and my meal plans, she started to get a little better. Then she got a lot better. And her hair even grew back!

Once we realized that Cousin Daisy was going to live after all, Bessie and I had a little talk. Bessie said, "Sadie, now that you've saved Cousin Daisy, you are responsible for her life." So I sent those vitamins, plus twenty dollars a month for food, until Cousin Daisy died. She lived to be an old woman. I think she was eighty-three years old when she passed on.

It's only now that I'm telling anyone about how I helped Cousin Daisy. I never told anyone at the time, except Bessie. The way we were brought up, it was only natural for Bessie and me to help other people. It wasn't something you did so that people thought well of you.

No, you did it because that was what was expected of you. It was the example that was set by the Good Lord, Jesus. It was also the example set by Mama and Papa.

23

BESSIE

In April 1928, Lemuel sent a telegram, "Come home quick, Papa's very ill." I thought, Lord have mercy, we're going to lose him. It was a shock. None of us had died in a long, long time and I guess we thought none of us ever would.

I did not get to Raleigh in time to see Papa. He had died, peacefully, at home. I saw his body, and the only thing that looked like my Papa was his hands. He had beautiful hands, and when I saw those hands I realized it was true, that he was gone from this Earth.

All my brothers came, and for a long time, people remembered how those six Delany boys — three on each side — carried Papa's coffin to the chapel. They were tall, good-looking boys and it was quite a sight, the way they lifted Papa's coffin up on their shoulders.

Now, you can imagine that poor Mama was mourning and grieving like the world was coming to an end. I remember telling her — she was a good-looking woman even then — that it would be OK by me if she wanted to remarry someday. She said, "I've had my husband, and I don't want another one, 'cause there's no one else that can compare."

Now that Papa was gone, Lemuel was the only one left in Raleigh, and so Mama wanted to be with the bunch of us in New York. I'm sure Mama had mixed feelings about leaving Raleigh, because other than her hometown outside Danville, Virginia, she had never lived anywhere else. She had been there for almost fifty years, living right on the campus of Saint Aug's where she had been a college student back in the 1880s.

I stayed behind in Raleigh to help Mama pack her things, which was very hard, since she had so many belongings and memories to let go of. The worst part was the day she said she wanted to burn all of her love letters to Papa. He had tied them up with a ribbon in a neat little bundle. I didn't want her to burn those love letters, but Mama's just like me, you can't talk her out of anything. So I watched from the window while she built a fire outside, and then read each letter, and put it in the fire. And these little black bits of ashes would blow around her. Lord, it was awful. I wouldn't relive that day for anything.

Fortunately, I had persuaded her to keep Papa's papers that were less personal, papers from his years as a teacher and clergyman. I packed them in suitcases and instructed my brother Hubert to carry them up to New York. But Hubert became so attached to those papers that Mama and I could not get them away from him. I would say to him, "Hubert, you give me those papers." And he would say, "Oh Bessie, I can't give them up. I just enjoy looking at his papers so much." This was an ongoing fuss that Hubert and I had until he died recently, when he was just shy of ninety years old. Hubert was a darling little brother, but he certainly could be stubborn. Yes, sir!

There wasn't a soul in Harlem who didn't know my brother Hubert. He was very active in the NAACP. He was an assistant United States attorney for the Southern District of New York. He prosecuted five hundred cases and lost only two.

In 1929 Hubert ran for Congress in the Twenty-first Congressional District in Harlem. My dental office was his campaign headquarters, and they hung a banner, "Hubert Delany for Congress!" in the big plate-glass window looking out over Seventh Avenue. His campaign manager was William Kelly, the editor of the *Amsterdam News* and our family friend.

Hubert won the Republican primary, but he lost the general election. Still, he won the admiration of Fiorello La Guardia, who sort of took him under his wing. Mayor La Guardia appointed Hubert as Tax Commissioner for the Borough of Manhattan in 1934, and Justice of the Domestic Relations Court in 1942. I remember during the 1935 race riot in Harlem that Hubert and Mayor La Guardia walked through the streets to try to quiet things down.

Hubert may have been the most famous of my

brothers, but they all followed in my Papa's foot-steps, becoming good family men with successful careers — real leaders of the community. Papa was such an excellent role model for his children. I could understand Hubert's attachment to Papa's papers because all of us felt the same way. Why, I'd be nothing without my Papa!

24

SADIE

Papa's death hit me hard; it hit us all hard. I didn't realize how safe I felt in this world because of Papa. Even after I moved to New York, I knew that somehow he was watching out for me. But even as a grown woman, forty years old or more, I was still something of a mama's child. I loved to be in the company of my Mama and I would just do anything for her.

While Papa was still alive, Mama had never seen much of the world at all. She had the whole world on her shoulders as the bishop's wife and being the matron at Saint Aug's. So after she moved up to New York, she was ready to go places. Even when she was very elderly, all you had to do was say, "Let's go," and she'd say, "Just let me get my hat."

Some of the happiest days of my life were going on trips with Mama — especially when we went abroad in the summer of 1930. We signed up for a tour that was run by a white man in Washington, D.C., who had a lot of colored clients. There were about a dozen people, half of us colored, who signed up for this particular trip. We took a ship out of New York and went to London, then on to Germany, Italy, France, Russia, Lithuania, Estonia, and Latvia. I suppose this man who ran our tour knew exactly where to take us because we had no incidents in which people mistreated us because we were colored.

The most memorable moment of the trip came in London, when we went to see Paul Robeson* in *Othello*. Paul's performance in the play was legendary, because he interpreted Othello from the perspective of a Negro man, which was a very important breakthrough in the history of theater. When Paul heard Mama and I were there, he was ecstatic. He had us brought backstage right away. He said it was so good to see some Delanys from Harlem! He seemed a little homesick.

Bessie knew Paul before I did. She knew him back at Columbia, before he became famous. I remember that once, years later, Bessie went to see him at the hospital in New York when he was sick. They weren't letting anyone in, but when he heard Bessie was there, he wanted to see her. And she just went in and held his hand.

Paul Robeson was not treated well in his later years. A lot of people thought he was a traitor to

* Paul Robeson (1898–1976) was a brilliant American actor and an outspoken advocate for civil rights. He was also a lifelong admirer of the Soviet Union. After a decades-long career in which he was revered, Robeson was blacklisted when Cold War-era anti-Communist sentiment turned many Americans against him.

our country, because he had gone to Russia. Well, Paul had made a film in Russia and was surprised to find that people there were not as racist, and he said so publicly. So what? He had the right to criticize America. All of us have that right.

When Mama and I were in Russia, after visiting London, we thought it was a most interesting country, but poor. I remember maids admiring our clothes at a hotel. And I remember that we were served cabbage soup at a hotel, and Mama and I laughed because in the South that is known as "pot liquor." I wanted to go out and buy us some fruit, but it was so expensive — a ruble for a single pear.

Then, in 1932, Mama and my little sister Laura and I went with Hubert and a man friend of his by car out to Los Angeles to see the Olympics. Los Angeles was sunny and clean, and you could hop in the car and go to the beach in no time. It took us a few days to understand the climate. We learned the hard way that it was cold in the morning, but would get hot as a stove by midday. At first we were dressed all wrong, but we got the hang of it.

We would get up early in the morning and go to the Olympic events all day long. I especially loved the track-and-field meets. We were proud of the achievements of the Negro athletes, and it was very inspiring to see them represent America.

One thing that I loved about California is the fruit you could buy there — oranges and things — for next to nothing. And there were all these strange-looking, beautiful plants growing every which way. Why, in California, poinsettias grew like *trees*. I would have moved to California, but Bessie wouldn't come with me. Bessie said she could never live anywhere where she would have to worry about the ground moving under her feet. Bessie likes her own two feet planted on the ground.

When we drove out to Los Angeles, we went the northern route across the U.S. — through the Great Plains — but on the way back, we went the southern route. We wanted to see as much of our country as we possibly could. But in the South, Hubert was worried that a carload of well-dressed Negroes from New York in a big, shiny car would attract the kind of attention we didn't need. He talked to people ahead of time about where to stay, and where not to stop, so we didn't run into any problems.

In cities we stayed in the best hotels. You reduced the chances of having trouble from white folks by staying at the best hotels. And in the country-side, we stayed in little roadside motels, and people were eager to take our money because the Depression was going on. When white folks were hungry, they'd overlook the fact that you were colored just to get your money.

The other reason we did not have trouble on that trip through the South was that we were light. I was light, Mama was light, Hubert was light, and so was his friend. Laura was a little darker, but she had straight hair. People knew we were

Negroes, but they weren't as likely to bother you if you were lighter. I suppose if Bessie had been with us, we might have had a little trouble. She's not only darker, she's feisty!

It was very rare that Bessie would go on vacation with Mama and me. It was harder for her to get away, because she would have to get Hap or someone else to look after her patients. Even her patients used to say to her, "Dr. Bessie, don't you ever go on vacation?" That gal worked day and night.

Well, she finally agreed to go with me to Atlantic City, where we stayed in a little colored rooming house. It was just full of bedbugs. We spent half the vacation getting rid of those bedbugs. It seemed like everywhere we went in our life, we always had to get rid of bedbugs!

I don't believe that the beach was segregated. If it was, then we were in the wrong place, because we were surrounded by white folks on the beach. But that was the difference between the North and the South. If that had been the South, they'd have thrown you on out of there if you didn't belong. In the North, you could get away with more.

Another popular vacation resort in those days was Niagara Falls. Mama had her heart set on going up there, so of course I took her. To get a good view of the falls, we went up in a biplane — you know, one of those open-top little airplanes they had in those days. We sent a postcard to Bessie, and she just blew her top! When we got back, she chewed me out good. She said to me, "What on Earth were you thinking, letting Mama go up in that biplane? She's an old lady!"

But you know, if Mama had her mind set on doing something, you couldn't stop her. And it sure was a beautiful view of Niagara Falls from up there; I will never forget it. It was like being a bird, flying through the sky. I turned around and looked back at Mama, and she was just sitting there, smiling. She was having the time of her life, and that made me so very happy.

25

BESSIE

Let me tell you a little story. Down South, somebody asked an old Negro man why he wouldn't fly in an airplane. And this is what he said:

"When you're in a train and it breaks down, well, there you is. But when you're in a plane and it breaks down, there you *ain't*."

That's exactly how I feel, honey! I never did like to fly in airplanes. That's why I was so annoyed by Sadie, taking Mama up in that biplane over those waterfalls! Mama must have been seventy years old at the time. What on Earth were they thinking? I think Sadie should have talked Mama out of it.

Mama and Sadie were always going off on these trips together. It worried me to death, getting these letters and postcards from those two, from who-knows-where. But they were natural travelers. Now me, I like to sleep in my own bed at night, bathe in my own bathtub, eat my own food.

In 1932 I took the one big trip of my life. A patient of mine, Mary Watson, invited me to visit her homeland, Jamaica. We went by boat. I'll tell you a secret about traveling by boat, honey. One of my patients said before I left, "Dr. Bessie, you won't get seasick if you fold a newspaper across your stomach and tie a piece of string around your waist to hold it up." Now, I thought that was the silliest thing I ever heard. But when my patient said, "I'll pay for your trip if it doesn't work!" I realized he meant business.

Well, we got in a terrible storm on that trip, and everybody on the boat got sick as a dog. Except me. I had a newspaper tied around my stomach! Me and the captain, we were the only two people who ate our dinner that night.

The boat stopped overnight in Cuba on the way to Jamaica. We got off and had dinner with an old beau of my Mama's, a Cuban Negro who had attended Saint Aug's. I remember that the houses came right up to the street in Cuba. The homes did not have porches, which seemed a crime to me.

The next morning we went on to Jamaica, and oh, what a beautiful place that was. But you know, it was different racially from America. In Jamaica, there were two official classes of Negroes: white Negroes and black Negroes. The white Negroes were higher class and had more privileges in society.

Now, my friend, Mary, was a very dark-skinned girl. Another one of my patients had said to me, "Dr. Bessie, don't go to Jamaica with her. You'll have problems." I didn't know what he was talking about.

Well, because I was lighter-skinned than Mary, I was treated like royalty by the higher-class Negroes. I was a brown-sugar-skinned gal, and that was acceptable. I wasn't *black,* and I was a dentist, from New York, and they all wanted to meet me. So all these invitations came to me from these elite Negroes, inviting me to dinner and to their clubs — invitations just for me.

Mary came from a lovely family — her parents were both teachers — but they were shunned by the white Negroes. I thought this was rude beyond belief. So I turned all those invitations down. I would write a note back and say, "No thank you, but I am a guest of Mary Watson, and I think it would be inappropriate for me to be your guest without her presence as well." My trip lasted several weeks, and finally, they wore down, and invited Mary, and so we went! So you see, I helped break some of these elite clubs in Jamaica.

Mary's family lived in a lovely home, and everything was made of mahogany. They had maids and servants, and those folks would polish the floors every day with a coconut. They would cut it open and rub it on the floor. I'll tell you another thing about those coconuts: When I first got there, Mary showed me her "tree." She said it was *her tree.* I thought she meant she had planted it as a little child. But it turns out that in Jamaica — at that time anyway — when a child was born, it was a tradition to wrap the placenta around a coconut and bury it in the yard. It was said to make the tree grow strong and straight. And that was *your tree*. This seemed mighty peculiar to a little old gal from Raleigh, North Carolina.

Mary showed me the whole island, from top to bottom. We walked, rode bicycles, drove these old rutted roads — just like North Carolina — all around the island. It was a beautiful place, and very relaxing. They did everything the slow way. You could live to be a thousand! Mary's mother had a maid who would wash the family's clothing, and it took her forever to do it. And I said to Mary's mother, "She is very inefficient. Do you want me to show her how to wash the clothes in one day?" And Mary's mother said to me, "No, it's OK. This is Jamaica. That's the way we do things here."

I'll tell you another thing about Jamaica that I learned: It was a poor place, a very poor place. The poor folks were the poorest I'd ever seen, and that includes those backwoods folks in the South, when I was teaching. I remember when we pulled in the harbor, all these children were diving in the water. I thought they were just having a good time. And Mary said, "No, they're diving for pennies. They're looking for pennies that the tourists throw for them into the water." Now, that just about broke my heart.

I carried around these two-and-a-half-dollar gold pieces that I brought along as little gifts, and I gave them all away in a hurry. On my way to the boat to go home, there was a man — a Negro man, black as your shoe — who was begging. He grabbed my arm, and said, "Oh, please can't you give me a little something." Well, I had given away all of my gold pieces and I didn't have anything left. I felt so bad.

But not long after I came back to the States, I had money problems of my own. The Depression was getting deeper and deeper, and money got tighter and tighter. Then, one day I was walking down the street in Harlem and I started to notice something funny. I saw all these papers just blowing down the street. I remember thinking, Wonder what that's all about. And I reached down and grabbed one of those pieces of paper, and do you know what? They were *my papers*. They were records from my dental office. I had been dispossessed.

I ran all the way to my office and found that the landlord had put all my things in boxes and just left them on the sidewalk. And the wind was just a-carrying everything away. We were behind on the rent. Hap got thrown out, too!

One thing about us Delanys: They used to say we were 99 percent nigger and one percent mule. We were the stubbornest things alive. We just kept a-going, no matter what. Well, as soon as Hap and me could scrape up the money for the rent we moved right back in. Well, what do you think happened? The landlord threw us out again, about a year later, for the same reason. But we always got back on our own two feet, yes, sir.

Sadie was not too affected by the Depression. You'd think everyone would be devastated by the Depression, and that was pretty much true. But

Sadie was a teacher with the New York City Board of Education. She had a steady paycheck through the entire Depression.

Now me, I was in a different situation. My patients had no money to pay me. Things were bad enough for most colored folks, before that Great Depression roared in like some old hurricane. You know, when times are good for white people, things are tolerable for colored folks. But when times are *bad* for white people, well, look out! Negroes are the first ones to suffer, yes, sir! Like in the South, after the Surrender — Papa said colored folks had it the worst. You can count on it, honey.

When that old stock market crashed, the next thing you knew, the world was falling apart. The newspapers were full of stories of rich white men who had committed suicide, jumping out of buildings, things like that. I can't imagine having so little faith in the Lord, and so much faith in money, that you would end your life over a little thing like losing your fortune. The Lord says money is Evil, and He is right! Money is the root of every mess you can think of, including slavery. Greed! Profiting off the backs of others!

Well, a lot of these white folks were *lost* without their big money, when that Great Depression hit. And they didn't have a clue how to live through hard times. Us Negroes, well, we knew what it was like to hit bottom, anyway. For my people, hardship was a way of life. The Great Depression was just another crisis.

No matter how bad things got, I never actually went hungry. I have not been without food for a single day in my life. Sadie and Mama would cook a meal for almost nothing, that is the truth. You never saw people who can live cheaper than we can.

In fact, I *fed* people during the Depression. My patients would show up and say, "Dr. Bessie, I'm *hungry*." and I'd always give them something, a piece of bread or whatever I had for myself. You just lived day to day.

I remember one of my patients saying to me, "Dr. Bessie, I have no shoes." That gal was walking around with rags on her feet. And I didn't have any money to give her. I said, "Well, I wish I could help you, but look at *my* feet." And I showed her the bottom of my shoes. I was walking around with cardboard in my shoes because I plumb wore out the soles.

Sadie was a little more practical about helping folks than I was. Sadie helped many, many people — one person at a time. But me — well, I always had everybody's problems on my shoulders, and honey, sometimes I struggled to carry that load. A patient of mine said to me once, "Your office isn't a dentist's office. It's a social service agency!" Yes, that was true.

Once, I gave a patient my radio. Now, I loved my radio. But this patient lived alone and was very poor, and I knew how much it would mean to her. I thought, How can I listen to my radio knowing that she could be enjoying it, even more than

I would? So I gave her that radio.

Sometimes I got in over my head. Lord, I never knew when to draw the line. One day, one of my patients came to me in tears. And I said, "Why, what is the matter?" She told me she was pregnant, and did not want the child. She had two other children and they were half-grown. She said, "Oh, Dr. Bessie, I can't afford to feed another child. I am going to have an abortion." That was illegal then, of course, but you could still get it done.

She cried and cried. And I blurted out, "Don't do it! Why, I'll raise that child! If you carry that child, I will even pay the doctor! And then I will raise that child myself!"

Whatever possessed me to say that, I don't know. I thought, Well, now I've really gone and gotten myself into a mess. What in the world was I going to do with a child on my hands? Well, I would have stuck to what I said, but being a little psychic, I had a hunch that once this woman had the baby she would not give it up. And what do you think happened? One day, just before she dropped that baby, she said, "Oh, Dr. Bessie, will you ever forgive me? I just can't give you this baby. I can't give it up!" Lord, was I ever relieved! But the truth is, I would have raised the child, somehow.

It turned out to be a little baby girl, and she was named Bessie, after me. And when little Bessie grew up, her mama told her what had happened, and little Bessie has always been grateful to me. Once she told me that I was like a second mother to her. She said there are things she could tell me that she could not tell her mother.

Sometimes, to this day, my doorbell will ring, and there is Bessie with a pail and some rags, and she just shows up and cleans all my knickknacks, cleans up my house. I can't stop her. At Christmas, she puts me and Sadie in her car and drives us around New York City to see the lights, takes us to Harlem to see all our old stomping grounds. So you can see why I call her my daughter. People who don't know nothing about my courting days — don't know I lived a clean life — they kind of raise their eyebrows when I talk about my "daughter." But I don't care.

I kept my practice going during the Depression, although now I wonder how I did. Then one day, in the middle of the Depression, one of my patients went to sign up for help from the government, and she asked me to go along to keep her company. They gave her some kind of little job. And I wasn't planning on this at all, but I said, "Say, do you have anything for me? I am a licensed dentist and I'm not doing so well myself." Well, next thing I knew, the government agreed to set up a clinic near City Hall, with me running it. And so I worked there in the mornings, for the rest of the Depression, for a small salary. And in the afternoon I would go back to my office and work there. So the government helped, but it wasn't no handout, no, sir! Let me make that clear. It was work-for-hire. I have never taken a handout from the government in my life.

I am the kind of Negro that most white people don't know about. They either don't know, or maybe they don't *want* to know, I'm not sure which. I mean, just listen to that fella, David Duke, down in Louisiana — the fella that was with the Klan and then he was going to run for president. David Duke doesn't think there are Negroes like me and Sadie, colored folks who have never done nothin' except *contribute* to America. Well, I'm just as good an American as he is — *better!*

Yes, I think I'm going to write a letter, and I'm going to say, "Dear Mr. Duke: This is just to set the record straight. I am a Negro woman. I was brought up in a good family. My papa was a devoted father. I went to college; I paid my own way. I am not stupid. I'm not on welfare. And I'm not scrubbing floors. Especially not yours."

PART VI
TIES THAT BIND

The stock market crash of October 1929 seemed remote to many residents of Harlem, like a foreign war being waged at the faraway tip of Manhattan Island. By the early 1930s, however, newspaper accounts indicate that the Great Depression had devastated Harlem. There were four or five times more unemployed people in Harlem than in any other section of New York.

Now legendary night spots like the Cotton Club took on a new civic role — raising money for food baskets for the poor — and jazz musicians were left struggling as the smaller clubs went under. The Harlem literary Renaissance collapsed altogether, with only Langston Hughes, of the original major writers, continuing for many years to live and write in Harlem. In the economic crisis, one artistic movement seemed to flourish: painting and sculpture, with Romare Bearden and Jacob Lawrence emerging as major figures of the era.

As the Depression deepened, evictions from offices and apartments occurred on every block with alarming regularity. Even the staff of the Brotherhood of Sleeping Car Porters, the powerful Negro union of railroad workers, was put out on the streets. It was not uncommon to see entire families digging through garbage for scraps of food. Government work programs brought some relief, but Harlem, along with the rest of the country, did not recover until America had entered World War II, which spurred a manufacturing boom and stimulated the economy.

Harlemites embraced World War II with the same patriotic fervor as the rest of the nation. A generation earlier, World War I had sparked protests in Harlem by black Americans who were angered that they were asked to fight overseas while they were treated as second-class citizens at home. World War II brought resentment because the armed forces remained segregated and because civilian munitions jobs were mostly closed to blacks. Still, the *Amsterdam News* and other black newspapers were filled with accounts of Harlem's aid to the war effort: Women knitted socks and sweaters for the troops, volunteers worked as air-raid wardens, and just about everyone who could find a few yards of unpaved earth grew a "Victory garden."

It was an anxious time, and all eyes were on Europe, Africa, and Asia. For the Delany sisters, however, an unfolding personal tragedy kept their focus very much at home.

26

SADIE AND BESSIE

By this time we had a heap of nieces and nephews and we loved them all dearly. But one of them, Little Hubie, had a special place in our hearts. He was what we called a spastic child. He was damaged when he was born. Little Hubie was the greatest tragedy of our lives.

When we were growing up, there were a lot of children born sickly. Children who were damaged were not institutionalized the way they are today. At least, among colored families, that was the way it was. We don't know about white folks. But among colored folks, you took care of your own.

There was a little girl at Saint Aug's who was born damaged. This little girl's name was Adelaide, and she was the only child of a music teacher named Mrs. Johnson. Well, Mrs. Johnson always invited us over to the house to play with Adelaide, although that child couldn't walk, and the only sounds she could make were these grunting and squealing noises. But I guess Mrs. Johnson thought it would be good for Adelaide if we spent time there, so we did. But there was always this feeling, from the way Mrs. Johnson looked at us, that she saw in us what she wished little Adelaide had been.

Mrs. Johnson's husband was also devoted to Adelaide. He was an attorney — one of the first, if not the very first, Negro attorneys in Raleigh. Every night, he would carry Adelaide downstairs to their dinner table — even when she was a big girl — and he would hold her in his arms while he fed her, one spoonful at a time. She had to be coaxed to eat, and he would sing and talk to her until he could get her to eat.

We had never had anyone in our family that was damaged like that until Little Hubie was born. He was our sister Julia's only child. About ten years earlier, Julia had followed Bessie and me to New York. She was a gifted musician, and graduated from Juilliard School of Music. Her specialty was piano, and that is what she taught when she graduated from college.

Julia always had an eye for very attractive men. We would say to her, "Now, Julia, you really must look for qualities beyond appearance." But she just couldn't help herself. Fortunately for her, she married a man who was good-looking who *also* happened to be nice. His name was Cecil Bourne, and he was a photographer. A good-looking photographer.

Well, Julia and Cecil wanted a family, but Julia had a very hard time. She became pregnant with twins, which they took from her because she nearly died. She was very, very ill. So when she became pregnant again, we were happy for her but scared. We all told the doctor that Julia was to come first. And when the baby came, he was big, and the doctor used forceps. The baby, Hubert Delany Bourne — we always called him "Little Hubie" — was born damaged.

At first, Julia didn't see that the baby was damaged. But by the time he was one year of age, we knew he was not a normal child. Little Hubie couldn't walk, so Julia pushed him around in a carriage.

Still, he was a very beautiful child and easy to love; he was very charming in his own way. Why, people said they never saw a child with such beautiful, expressive eyes. Cecil took roll after roll of film of that baby.

Little Hubie also had a very active mind. His cousin, Harry M. Delany, who today is a medical doctor in New York City, was the same age as Little Hubie. Harry was a very bright little boy, but one time we were giving him a spelling lesson and he spelled a word incorrectly. Little Hubie was sitting nearby and he banged his hand on the table and shook his head. He knew that Harry had spelled it wrong!

Another time, Julia was worried about a drug the doctors prescribed to help Little Hubie sleep at night. She was afraid he would become an addict. But we were more worried that Little Hubie was becoming weakened by not getting his sleep. We said, "Julia, don't deprive that poor child of his medicine." And Little Hubie, in this funny way of talking he had, said, "That's right. Give that poor child his medicine. Don't let him suffer." That child didn't miss a trick.

Since Julia was our sister, we tried to help her with Little Hubie any way we could. We tried to deal with the problem the way we always did, as a family. We prayed a great deal, and we did not give up.

We had Little Hubie enrolled in a program that was probably the best in the world at that time for little spastic children. It was at Columbia, actually a school at the hospital for these children. The instructor gave us great hope, because he himself was spastic but had managed to grow up and live a full life. We thought, If he can do it, then Little Hubie can, too. What we didn't grasp was that spastic people are damaged in different ways. Hubie had problems that no one could diagnose or treat.

We always included Little Hubie in family outings, even on dates with our boyfriends. Nobody thought this was strange. People were very family-oriented in those days. Bessie's boyfriend Dean was particularly fond of Little Hubie.

One day Bessie asked him, "You think Little Hubie is going to be all right, don't you, Dean?" She was really looking for him to agree with her, you know. But he didn't answer and looked away. She asked again, chilled to the bone. She said, "Answer me, Dean. You do think Little Hubie will be all right, don't you?" And he finally said, "No, Bessie, I do not."

It had just never occurred to us that Little Hubie would die. We all had this idea that he would be all right some day. We just thought that with enough prayer, enough love, and enough determination we would overcome this. But it wasn't part of God's plan. It was a shock to us.

It wasn't long after that when Little Hubie began to slip away. It was pneumonia that finally took him from us. He was ten years old when he died. The date was the seventh of March, 1943. To this day, we always celebrate his birthday on the tenth of June. Bessie still has his blanket on her bed, and sleeps with it every night.

Little Hubie's death humbled us. We were sort of cocky before that. We thought we could do anything, fix any problem. We were not afraid of adversity. We were Delanys! After Little Hubie, we realized you can't always get what you want in life.

27

SADIE AND BESSIE

You can get very close to God, tilling the soil. When the government asked people to grow Victory gardens to help the war effort, we were only too happy to oblige. We knew it would help us get over Little Hubie.

During World War II, we moved to 80 Edgecombe Avenue, a very fashionable section of Harlem, on a street with beautiful brownstones. It was a brick building, six stories high, with tile floors in all the hallways and hardwood floors in the apartments. There was no doorman, but the front door was kept locked, and there were mailboxes inside, in the lobby. There were little luxuries, like windows on the side apartments. It must have been built for white people.

A lot of the Negro elite lived in that building. For instance, A'Leilia Walker Robinson, the daughter of Madame C. J. Walker, one of the first colored millionaires, lived there at one time. We felt lucky to get an apartment there. Ours was on the second floor.

But there really was no room to grow a substantial garden on the grounds of 80 Edgecombe. So our cousins in the Bronx said it would be OK to use a vacant lot next to their property. We went up there as often as we could, and grew the best Victory garden in the neighborhood.

World War II meant shortages of everything, like gasoline and sugar. We were in the habit of taking public transport, so the gasoline rationing didn't hurt us too much. But that sugar shortage was living Hell for us. The only way you could get enough sugar to make sweets was to hold candy-pull parties. We would invite all our friends to bring their ration of sugar and we would make a batch of candy. And we would make a party, just eating all that candy.

We Delanys were as patriotic as anyone. We were Americans! Our blood and sweat was invested in this land, and we were ready to protect it. As bad as things were for Negroes, you wouldn't have wanted to live anywhere else in the world, that's for sure.

Negroes are used to getting kicked around, so we can sympathize when other people get picked on. Like when they sent Japanese-Americans to those internment camps; now, that was wrong! That was racial paranoia. And when the news came out about those concentration camps, we felt so sorry for the Jews and the Gypsies and all those folks. Mankind can be cruel beyond words. Yes, we colored folks can relate to that, because we've surely had folks who wanted to stomp on us, tried to wipe us out.

During World War II in New York, life revolved around the news. There were many newspapers, not just three or four like today. And we would try to keep up with what battle was happening where, and how many casualties.

Our brother Manross had made a career of the army and so he was swept right up in World War II. He helped build the Burma Road. Now, Manross had an experience during World War II that made him very bitter, very angry. The army was still segregated then, but Manross's unit had been situated near a white unit, and somehow Manross saved some white fella's life. This white fella was also from North Carolina, and when Manross told him he was going home soon on leave, his new buddy told him to be sure to stop by and see his folks. Well, when poor Manross got there, he knocked on the door, but those white folks wouldn't let him in. They didn't want their neighbors to see a Negro coming to their front door! They told him to go around to the *back*.

If some white boy had showed up on our door-step and said he was a friend of Manross's — that he had rescued Manross from death — do you think we would have told him to go around to the back? Manross was very deeply hurt by that experience.

Now, we had nephews who were in World War II also. One of Hap's sons got himself in a heap of trouble in the army. This boy was born and raised in Harlem, so we had worried about him being in boot camp down in Texas. Northern Negroes sometimes just didn't know how to get along in the South.

Well, that boy talked back to some white sergeant and ended up being thrown in jail. Eventually, he was court-martialed. *Can you imagine?* He was a smart boy and very patriotic, just inexperienced about dealing with the rebby boys in the South, that's all. The whole thing was quite a mess. Our family had to get Adam Clayton Powell* to intervene, and we got our nephew back, but he did not have a long life. And we always wonder if the experience hadn't broken his health and his spirit.

When the war ended, people went wild in New York. We went to church and prayed. Thank the Lord, the war was finally done! It was a terrible, terrible thing, though, that they used that bomb. They said the war would have dragged on forever without it. But it was like Man had lost his mind altogether, that day.

After the war was over, we didn't want to give up our Victory garden. We started thinking about moving from Harlem to the Bronx. Why, wouldn't it be nice to live where Mama could have a garden? Wouldn't it be nice to get Mama out of an apartment?

* Adam Clayton Powell Jr. (1908–1972) was minister of the Abyssinian Baptist Church in Harlem from 1937 to 1960, following in the footsteps of his famous father, Adam Clayton Powell Sr. Using the church as his political base, the younger Powell, who was a flamboyant and controversial figure, won election to Congress in 1944 and gained a reputation as the premier civil rights legislator in the nation.

Well, that's exactly what we did. We bought a little cottage in the North Bronx, next to where we had our Victory garden. There was lots of vacant land there, then, and trees and shrubs. It was like the country.

The first thing we did was to hire a man to put a porch on our little cottage. He laughed at us. He said, "You're going to put a porch on that little old two-room cottage?" And we were very annoyed at him. We said, "Mister, we're from North Carolina and we've been cooped up in apartments since the First World War. Now we've got this cottage out in the country, and where we're from, a house ain't a home unless it has got itself a porch!"

So we got ourselves a porch. And it meant that no matter how bad the weather, we were able to make sure Mama got her walk every day. Mama was getting very elderly, getting on ninety years old, and we wanted her to live forever. So we made sure she got her exercise every day. When the weather was nice, we would each take her by the arm, on either side, and we would walk around the neighborhood. By this time, we were getting older ourselves. One little boy yelled at us, "Look, *three* grandmas going for a walk." We thought it was funny. But it was true, we were getting old, too.

Soon, we started having trouble keeping Mama in line. Our little cottage was equipped only with propane gas, and we were afraid Mama would burn herself up. When we left for our jobs in the morning, we would say, "Now, Mama, don't you go cooking a hot meal while we're away." And when we'd come home, she'd have a hot meal ready for us. She didn't listen to us one bit.

And another thing Mama would do: She would give money to strangers. And we would say, "Now, Mama, this is not North Carolina. You can't go talking to people you don't know." But she would do it, just like when we were children and Uncle Jesse and all the hoboes would come by, and she would always fix them a plate of food.

One day, we came home and Mama seemed all shook up. She refused to tell us what happened, but we think she was robbed or roughed up. All we know is that after that day, she finally listened to us. She stopped letting people into the house.

Mama also kept losing her pension check. She started hiding it, and then she couldn't find it. And she wouldn't like to admit that she had lost it. So she would wait until no one was around except Sadie. Then she would come up to Sadie and whisper, "I have misplaced my check. Can you help me find it?" And Sadie would always say, "Of course I'll help you find it, Mama." Sometimes they'd have to take the whole house apart to locate that check. It was getting so we couldn't count on Mama's judgment anymore.

It got so that we would rush home from our jobs in fear, every day. Finally, we decided that one of us was going to have to quit working and take care of Mama. What else could we do?

28

BESSIE

Well, it was obvious that I was the one who should quit my job, even though Sadie was a mama's child. We sat down and thought it through, financially. If Sadie continued to work until 1960, she would get $150 a month from her pension with the New York City Board of Education. She said, "That would be $50 for Mama, $50 for you, and $50 for me." She was going to just split it three ways. We figured that the three of us, living together, could do OK on $150 a month. And Mama got $15 a month from Papa's pension. Mama was so funny about that $15. She was so proud of it, you'd have thought it was fifteen *million*.

I was a dentist, working independently, and I had no pension plan. So it was settled. I was to close my practice. Truth is, I was only fifty-nine years old and I had planned to work for many years yet. But once the decision was made, I accepted it.

I remember being at a dinner party just before I retired. There was a woman there, a very flashy, important Negro at that time. And she said to me, in front of all these people, "You're going to give up your *career* to take care of your *mama!?*" And I said, "Honey, let me tell you something. If you had my Mama you wouldn't think *twice*." And that's really the way I felt.

I was never much of a housekeeper. I was not a natural talent. Sadie was better, of course, and my littlest sister, Laura — now that woman always knew how to make a perfect home. But I set out to make that little cottage nicer than it had ever been. I polished the brass fixtures in the bathroom until they gleamed. Why, one of my little nieces told the whole neighborhood that we had gold fixtures. They were so bright she thought they were gold.

Mama had been a perfect housekeeper and I thought that's what she wanted. She would say, "Bessie, why don't you just sit down here next to me?" And I would say, "In a minute, Mama, when I'm done shaking out the rugs," or whatever. But she didn't want brass fixtures that gleamed like gold; she wanted *me*. She was an old lady and she wanted her child to just sit with her, to be near her. Now that I am very old I understand this. I say to Sadie, "Whatever possessed me to try to make that little cottage perfect? Why didn't I just spend more time with Mama?"

Mama was still full of spunk, right up to the end. Why, one time my brother Hubert took Mama to the Statue of Liberty, and they raced each other down all those steps! I think Mama was ninety years old at the time. Well, when I heard about it I really let Hubert have it. I said, "What in the world were you doing, letting Mama run like that? What if she had a heart attack or something?" I was really steaming. He was a grown man. He was a judge, for Heaven's sake! I don't know what got into those two, but it was awfully silly.

But Hubert also gave Mama her greatest moment as an old lady. He had been the attorney and adviser for the singer Marian Anderson. That was back in 1939 when the Daughters of the American Revolution kept her from singing in Constitution Hall in Washington, just because she was colored. And then Mrs. Roosevelt intervened and arranged for Marian to sing at the Lincoln Memorial. Oh, that Mrs. Roosevelt was ahead of her time about equality of the races. To this day, we admire Eleanor Roosevelt more than any other famous person.

So, as a surprise for Mama, Hubert arranged for her to meet Eleanor Roosevelt! When we came into the room, there she was, and she jumped up like a jackrabbit to greet Mama, taking her hand. It was pretty wonderful to see the former First Lady of the United States jump up, so respectful-like, to greet Mama, an old colored lady.

Sadie and I were in charge of Mama's happiness, but all the children fussed over her. Once, in about 1950, our brothers got together and bought Mama a television set, which was a very rare thing in those days. We kept it quiet that we had a TV because we knew the whole neighborhood would be over at our house if they knew we had one. Mama sure got a kick out of watching Milton Berle.

We had a white doctor in the Bronx — there wasn't a Negro doctor near where we lived — and he used to say, "I've never seen anything like the way you Delanys look after your mother." When we first moved to the Bronx, our little brother Sam, who was an undertaker, would drop what he was doing and drive up there in a limousine to take Mama to her meetings at Saint Martin's Episcopal Church in Harlem, where she was president of the ladies' auxiliary. One time, one of the brothers — I won't say who — was naughty and hadn't been seeing enough of Mama. She came right out and told him she felt neglected. He said, "Why, Mama, is that really the way you feel?" She said yes, it was. So from that day until the day she died he visited her every single day, and if he was sick or away, he would send flowers or call her just to say hello. Mama was the queen bee.

When Mama was close to the end, she suddenly had this great need to tell me about her people. Of course, I had known her parents, Martha Logan and James Miliam, because I was a grown woman when they died. But I did not know much about those who came before them.

Up until this time, Mama was a little embarrassed that her parents were never married, even though they *couldn't* get married under Virginia law, as a white man and a colored woman. But

231

I don't think Mama was so ashamed anymore, once she got very old. I understand this now. When you get real old, honey, you realize there are certain things that just don't matter anymore. You lay it all on the table. There's a saying: Only little children and old folks tell the truth.

But hard times were coming. First, Manross died of a heart attack on November 3, 1955. When it happened, I called Lemuel on the telephone and I said, "Lemuel, sit down, I have some bad news." He said, "OK, I'm ready. It's Mama, isn't it?" He thought for sure I was going to tell him that Mama had gone. He said, "Manross? Manross? Manross?"

Losing Manross was a shock to all of us. He was the first of our generation to die, and we knew there would be more dying because we Delanys tend to die in threes. Strange thing is, it was Lemuel who went to Glory next. He died of a heart attack on January 9, 1956. Coming so soon after Manross had died, it was a terrible blow to poor Mama. She hadn't gotten over Manross yet, and I had to sit her down and tell her about Lemuel, and she cried and cried. I said, "Mama, try to pull yourself together." She wasn't just sad, she was kind of angry. I don't think she ever expected to outlive any of her children. After she lost Manross and Lemuel, I guess it was only natural that Mama was ready to go. But to tell you what a silly old gal I am, I have to admit I did not realize when Mama was leaving us. I did not realize my Mama was dying.

We knew it would have to happen eventually because, after all, Mama was ninety-five years old. The day it happened was the second of June, 1956. Mama had been ailing and stayed in bed that day. My nephew Lloyd was there visiting, and he was sitting at the foot of the bed, Sadie was sitting at the head of the bed, and I was just kind of hovering around. We noticed that Mama was breathing kind of heavy. Sadie whispered to Lloyd: "Is she dying?" And Lloyd said, "I think so."

Now, I misunderstood what they said to each other. Even with all my medical training, I didn't get what was going on! But Sadie knew; the mama's child could feel it in her bones. Silly me, I left the room and went out into the yard. It was getting dark and I wanted to feed my pet dogs and birds. Then Sadie came outside and said, "Bess, Mama's gone."

Well, in ten minutes' time all of the Delanys were swarming around our little cottage. The doctor came, and pronounced Mama dead. Our brother Sam, the undertaker, drove up from Harlem and scooped up Mama and carried her away. Our sister Julia climbed into Mama's bed and stayed there all night. She wouldn't come out.

Now, Sam called me from the funeral parlor and said, "Bess, why don't you come down here and fix Mama's hair?" You see, about a year or two before Mama died, she started complaining about how difficult it was for her to comb out her hair and fix it up nice every day. And I would say, "Mama, do you want me to take care of your hair for you?" I really didn't think she would say yes, because she was struggling so hard to stay independent, but she sighed and said, "That would be OK."

So, every day, from then on, I combed out Mama's hair every morning — she still kept it long — and I put it up on her head. She looked like Queen Victoria herself. So after she died, I went down to Sam's funeral parlor and did Mama's hair one last time. It made my heart bleed, but it seemed a nice way to say good-bye.

Bad as it was for me, Mama's death was ten times worse for Sadie. Poor Sadie just cried for weeks and weeks. Every time we sat down for a meal, with Mama's chair sitting there empty, the tears would come streaming down Sadie's face. Why, I wasn't sure she would make it. I thought she might die, too. Lord knows, she wasn't eating anything.

It's probably a good thing that Mama went to Glory when she did, because Sam, her baby, was getting real sick and it wasn't too long afterward that we lost him. He was only fifty-four years old when he died of lung cancer on October 1, 1960. Then, a few years later, on April 1, 1969, we lost Lucius, who had been having heart trouble, so we kind of expected that. But it was harder to swallow when Julia died in 1974, because her death was completely avoidable.

Julia died from taking penicillin. She had fallen in her kitchen and broken her hip, and she was taken to the hospital. It said right on her chart,

"No penicillin," and they gave it to her anyway, despite me protesting, along with other members of the family. I think Julia would have lasted a long time — maybe as long as me and Sadie — but they killed her at that hospital. That is the truth.

I don't think Mama would have been at all surprised that Sadie and I have kept living this long. We learned a lot from her about being old. Mama set a good example. She took care of herself, and she was surrounded by love.

I'll tell you something kind of funny. It had annoyed Mama that when Manross died, they made his wife return the pension check he had in his pocket. She thought that was mean. So she said, "If I die and I have a check in my pocket, Sadie, you must promise me that you will run to the bank and cash it, and keep that money!"

So, while Mama was ailing, Sadie did just that. And do you know that the pension company sent a letter immediately? They had seen Mama's obituary in *The New York Times* — that Bishop Delany's widow had died — and they sent a letter that said, "Please return the last check." And Sadie wrote to them, "Sorry, but it was cashed."

We always did what Mama asked.

29

SADIE

Now, you might ask, what happens to a mama's child when her Mama passes on? Well, it was worse than anything, except maybe when Little Hubie died. Little Hubie's death was a tragedy, because he didn't get much of a chance at living. We knew Mama would have to go to Glory sometime; she was a very old lady. So it wasn't like a real tragedy. Still, her passing hurt me something terrible.

I was so dependent on my Mama. Why, as a young girl, I remember my Mama had to go to see her parents for two weeks; maybe it was when her sister, Eliza, died. I was a plump child, and Mr. Hunter, the white principal of the school, was trying to help me to lose weight. Well, I lost eight pounds in those two weeks! And Mr. Hunter said to me, "Good heavens, child, what is wrong with you?" And I just burst into tears and said, "It's because my Mama has gone away!"

When I was a grown woman and moved up to New York, I wrote at least one letter every day to my Mama, back in North Carolina. Child, a day didn't go by that I didn't send her a letter, or sometimes two. And after Papa died, I was so glad Mama left Raleigh and moved in with me and Bessie. Until the day she died, Mama called me her "shadow." So when she died I thought, Maybe I should die myself. I guess I was — what's that word people use today? — depressed. Yes, that's the word. I think I was depressed. I was in a depression.

But Mama was gone, and I had to think about the world in a completely different way. Bessie says that for the first time in my life, I seemed to come into my own, as an individual person. I was sixty-seven years old.

Since our older brother Lemuel had died, and Papa had died long before, Mama's passing meant I was now the head of the family. There was never a family decision that didn't get brought to me for my opinion. This was hard on Bessie. It was easy for her to let Mama be the boss, but it was hard for her to play second fiddle to me. I think Bessie would prefer to be the boss! But she does listen to me. Not right away, all the time, but she will usually come around and say, "OK, you're older than I am, whatever you decide." I think it about kills her to say it, but she does.

Bessie and I just figured we would keep living at the cottage in the Bronx. We didn't have any other plans. But the neighborhood there was not what it had been. Even before Mama had died, things had gone downhill.

You see, they put this housing project in. Why,

the city had wanted to tear down our little cottage, and put the housing project there. But Bessie and I filed a lawsuit. We asked that they salvage our little cottage, move it across the street.

On the day it went to court, I was at school and couldn't get away. Bessie went to meet our lawyer at the courthouse, but he didn't show up. And you know what happened? Bessie just handled our side of things, by herself! She told the judge that the cottage was all we had in this world, and we wanted Mama to die there. And couldn't the city just move that old cottage across the street, to a vacant lot?

I guess she was convincing, because she won the case! But funny thing is, it got back to us that the judge was a bit miffed at Bessie. We heard later that he said, "That woman shook her finger at me! In *my* courtroom!" I guess he had never had that happen before. Well, that's my sister Bessie.

Now, when the day came for the city to move the house, they were very spiteful and mean. They moved it halfway. That's right! The workers left our little two-room cottage in the middle of the road overnight! They said, "You gals are going to have to find somewhere else to sleep tonight." Well, we slept there anyway, out of sheer stubbornness! One end of the house was up on jacks and the house was tilted at a weird angle, so our feet were above our heads when we went to sleep. Those men were astonished when they came the next day. It never occurred to them that we could

238

be that stubborn. Another thing: Bessie was so angry at those men that she took a crowbar that belonged to them and hid it. That thing is still in our basement! I think it gave Bessie some satisfaction to watch those silly men looking all over for that old crowbar. It is the only thing either one of us ever took from someone else in our whole lives. I'm not going to make any excuses for Bessie. She knows what she did. It's one of those things she's going to have to get straight with the Lord.

Anyway, they went and built this silly housing project, with us living right across the street from it. Some of the children from the housing project got into trouble. You can't just take people who don't have anything, don't know what they're doing, pack them in a bunch of buildings, and expect it's going to all work out somehow. No, it brought the neighborhood down.

Now, Bessie and I did not have trouble from those children. Everybody on our side of the street would get upset, because the children would do things like steal all the fruit from their fruit trees. And people would say, "Why don't those children bother *your* fruit trees?" The reason was that we were nicer to the children. We went out there and said to them, "The fruit on our peach trees isn't ripe yet, so please leave it alone. But when it is ripe, you come by and we'll share it with you." And we did. And those children never harmed us, or our trees or anything we owned.

The children from the housing project were white and colored, Christian and Jewish. I remember one time, a little Jewish boy heard me say some little quote from the Bible — from the New Testament — and he asked me to explain what it was all about. And I thought for a minute and then I said, "Child, you go home and ask your mama if it's OK for Miss Delany to tell you a story from the New Testament. If she tells you it's OK, then come on back." We were brought up to be respectful of other religions. Well, the boy's mother said it was fine. She said, "Anything those Delanys teach you is all right with me."

We loved the children in that neighborhood, but they were in our hair all the time. Part of it was our own fault. At Halloween, Bessie and I would make candied apples and homemade doughnuts, and the children went wild.

But we had no peace. We never had a meal at that cottage when we weren't interrupted. The doorbell would ring, and there would be a child there, wanting something. I remember once, it was a little boy holding a robin with a broken wing. And the child was crying, and hoping Miss Sadie and Dr. Bessie could fix that bird. I remember Bessie said to me: "It isn't the bird that needs attention as much as the *child*." We never denied those children the attention they needed, but it just about wore us out.

Then, one day, Bessie went to visit our brother Hap at his new home in Mount Vernon, in the suburbs. While she was there, Hap's wife, Audrey, put this idea in Bessie's head that maybe the two of us ought to get out of the Bronx and move into their neighborhood in Westchester.

Tell you the truth, we didn't think we could afford it. It was a white neighborhood. But then one day, Audrey told Bessie that the house at the end of the street was for sale. The old white lady who owned it had gone to the hospital for a minor operation but had died. Well, Audrey convinced Bessie to take a look. And Bessie came back home to me in the Bronx and said, "Sadie, I think we can do it. I think we must find a way to buy that house."

Bessie sat down and figured out how much the taxes were, and so on, and realized that we could do it, if we lived very, very cheap. So we went ahead and bought the house. We were really part of a group of Negroes who were beginning to leave the city. Middle-class Negroes like us, who could manage it.

Not only was our house at the end of a dead-end street, but it faced away from the other houses, with a view of New York City. There was plenty of room for a great, big garden, and since it was a two-family house, we moved into one side and rented out the other. For a long time, we had our own kin living next door, including our sister Laura and her husband, Ed, before they moved to California. So it has been a safe and peaceful little haven for us.

Bessie says now that she had an ulterior motive in moving us out of the Bronx. She says she didn't think I would ever get over Mama's death, and that maybe by moving away and starting over, it would help. I think she was right.

PART VII

OUTLIVING THE REBBY BOYS

The decades following the end of World War II were an era of new hope for black Americans. Under pressure from Congressman Adam Clayton Powell Jr. and A. Philip Randolph of the Brotherhood of Sleeping Car Porters, President Harry Truman desegregated the armed forces in 1948. Several years later, with the Supreme Court's ruling on *Brown v. Board of Education of Topeka, Kansas,* desegregation of schools became the law of the land.

Then, on December 1, 1955, a department store tailor named Rosa Parks singlehandedly assailed the Jim Crow laws by not giving up her seat to a white man on a bus in Montgomery, Alabama. Her protest sparked a revolution, spearheaded by the Reverend Martin Luther King Jr. — a decade of protests against racial discrimination at the voting booth, and in schools, employment, and public accommodations. Television cameras rolled as white lawmen beat back the protestors with clubs, dogs, and fire hoses. The demonstrators' slogan was, "The whole world is watching," and indeed, those images of violence would help secure passage of landmark civil rights legislation guaranteeing black Americans their full constitutional prerogatives.

But while the battle for integration was raging in the South, de facto segregation persisted in the North, often by subtle means that were hard to combat directly. Housing was one of the most visible arenas of struggle, as black people were frequently barred from moving into white neighborhoods. White resistance ran especially high in the new suburbs that rose after World War II and that offered a life-style that had begun to represent the American dream. And now the Delanys — entering retirement and so sidelined during the years of civil rights demonstrations — joined the advance guard of a different integration movement.

30

BESSIE

Today, all of Mount Vernon, it seems, is mostly Negro, but in 1957, it was mostly white. I don't think either Sadie or I had ever lived among so many white folks before, and it was a bit of a shock to us. Of course, we were a bit of a shock to *them*.

Hap had broken the neighborhood; he was the first colored person to move in there. They wouldn't let him buy a house. People blocked that. You know, the white real estate agents found excuses not to show him houses in certain neighborhoods, things like that. So do you know what Hap did? He *built* a house. He just went and bought a piece of land right smack in the middle of the nicest white neighborhood, and before the neighbors could figure out what was happening, they were pouring the foundation.

Hap had some trouble for a while, after they moved in. More than once, some white folks cut the tires on his Cadillac. But what those folks didn't understand was that Hap was a Delany, and the

247

harder they tried to push him out, the more he dug in his heels. But his experience did not discourage Sadie and me from moving there. We figured, Why shouldn't we live where we want to?

The first time I answered the door at our house in Mount Vernon, it was some white lady from Welcome Wagon and she went on and on about this and that and then she said to me, "And be sure you tell the owner . . ."

And I said, "Lady, I have news for you. I *am* the owner."

Well, she about dropped dead. It was clear she thought I was the *maid*. You know she was thinking, What's this little darkey doing, owning a big house like this? Or: Lord, this neighborhood is finished! It's doomed! The darkies have taken over! They'll bring all their friends!

Once, when we were new to the neighborhood, a white policeman came knocking on the door. We were a little afraid. What did he want from us? Well, we went upstairs, and opened the window and called down to him. That's what we do when we aren't sure about opening the door for someone. Sadie said to me, "Let me handle him." She leaned out the window and said:

"Officer, can I help you?"

And he called up: "We're raising money for the auxiliary, and I'm selling tickets to a dance."

And she giggled and said, "Why officer, thank you very much, but I'm too old to go to a dance!" And she giggled some more and shut the window.

Now, I just hate it when Sadie plays dumb like

that! I told her, "Sadie, that fella must think you're the dumbest nigger alive." And she said, "So what? I didn't make him angry, did I? And I've still got my money, don't I?" It annoys me, but I have to admit she was right.

Back when Negroes were starting to move into Mount Vernon, some of the white folks were mighty ornery. They would complain about such petty things, like the way that Negro children would play in the street. Well, those children didn't know any better. They had come from the city, and that's how children play in the city. It was little things like that, little cultural differences, that were the source of tension.

There is only one white family left in our neighborhood now. And you know, they recently had a terrible blow: Their son died tragically. He was about twenty years old. Now, that family had always been suspicious of us colored folks. I brought them some vegetables from my garden a long time ago and they made it clear they didn't want to be friends. They never thanked me or anything. They were pretty rude.

Now, when that boy died, they sure were surprised at how the colored folks reacted on the block. We just went on over there, quietly, and brought food and flowers. One thing about Negroes, we know how to react in a tragedy. We know how to show support. Do you know what? That white family sent every one of us a thank-you note. That surprised *us*.

Some white folks believe that Negroes bring

down a neighborhood because they don't keep up their property. Well, in our case, we had the neatest, spiffiest-looking yard on the block! Sadie and I set out to have the best garden you could find, and it has given us a great deal of pleasure. For many years, these little old white gals would walk over from this white retirement home, just to look at it, every day. Of course, we had lots of flowers, roses, you name it; but we also grew vegetables, like Kentucky wonder-beans, which we would eat or can for the winter months.

I'll tell you a funny thing that happened with our garden. A beautiful plant with a star-shaped leaf started growing there, and we couldn't figure out what it was. It annoyed us because we thought we knew everything about gardening and we hadn't seen this plant before. It got bigger and bigger, and we covered it faithfully each winter. Whenever we had visitors to the house, we would say, "Do y'all know what kind of plant that is?" And none of our visitors ever knew, either. Finally, our young nephew said, "Aunt Bessie! Aunt Sadie! What in the world are y'all doing with a marijuana plant in your garden?" Well, we surely were surprised. And I said, "Sadie, we had better get rid of it immediately, because we are breaking the law!" Don't worry, we got somebody to take care of it.

Our biggest problem with that old house was that we did not have the money to furnish it. We didn't want to go spending all our savings on furniture. We didn't know how long we would live, and we thought if we took after Mama and lasted a long time we would need that hard-time money in the bank, yes, sir!

So I'll tell you what we did. We started buying furniture from the Salvation Army. Now, we didn't mind having things secondhand. After all, we grew up wearing secondhand clothes that Mama bought at the missions store. In those days, rich people gave a lot of good furniture to the Salvation Army. Well, we learned real quick that they would always quote Sadie a high price.

So, we worked out a plan. We would go in the store together and scout out any good furniture they had just gotten there. And then we'd leave, kind of casually, to discuss what we should buy. Then, Sadie would go in and say, "How much do you want for that?" And they would give her a price like $15. Then, I'd go in, prepared, and say, "How much do you want for that old thing?" And they'd say, $15. And I'd say, "What? Fifteen dollars for that old piece of junk?" And they'd say, "Well, ten dollars." And I'd say, "I'll give you eight." And the next thing you knew, we had a big old piece of mahogany furniture — just what we needed — for eight dollars. We did this all the time, until we had all the furniture we needed.

Next to the Salvation Army was a day-old bread store. This became Sadie's job — to shop at the day-old bread store. She knew what was good and what was not, just by looking at it. And honey, we saved a ton of money over the years, shopping at that bread store. We ain't too proud to eat day-old bread!

It was while we were shopping at the Salvation Army and the day-old bread store that we heard that President Kennedy had been shot. They had a radio on in the Salvation Army and when I heard the news, I ran to the bread store and told Sadie: "They've done killed him." And she said, "Killed who?" It was such a shock, that someone would kill our young president like that. It made my heart bleed. Sadie and I believe it was the Mafia that did it.

After that, it seemed like all the leaders were getting shot — Malcolm X, Martin Luther King, Robert Kennedy. Sadie and I were so distressed about it. I'm glad that Ted Kennedy didn't run for president because I think he'd have gotten himself killed, too. Ted Kennedy has made some serious mistakes in his life, but Sadie and I decided he must be a nice boy because we heard on the radio that he visits his mother all the time up in Massachusetts. And Sadie says, "If he's nice to his Mama, then he's OK by me."

It's interesting the way folks have become interested in Malcolm X again. A lot of the things he said were true, but he said them so bluntly that white folks were scared to death of him. It was easier for white folks to admire Martin Luther King, because he was less threatening to them.

As far as Sadie and I are concerned, Martin Luther King was an angel. He just dropped from Heaven. And there hasn't been anyone as special since then. Now, I know that Martin Luther King was not perfect. There are all these stories coming out about him now; they may not be true at all. And if they are? Well, I never expected him to be perfect. He was a man, after all. I didn't expect him to be Jesus Christ.

One of the biggest regrets of my life was that Sadie and I didn't go to Washington for the big march in the summer of 1963. I would have loved to have heard Martin Luther King give his "I Have a Dream" speech. We were already old ladies at the time — in our seventies — and some younger relatives talked us out of going. They thought we'd be overwhelmed in those crowds.

It's a good thing we didn't go because the woman we had planned to go with did a silly thing. She was so determined to get near Martin Luther King that she got up as close as she could and then pretended to faint. They carried her over to the VIP tent, which is what she had in mind, I guess. Well, if Sadie and I had been separated from her, who knows what could have happened? We might have had trouble getting back to New York.

We had a lot of younger relatives involved in the civil rights movement of the '50s and '60s. We had one nephew who went down to Selma* and we were just worried to death. We saw all that action on the TV where they were turning fire hoses on those poor colored folks and, honey,

*The city of Selma, Alabama, was the site of a key series of civil rights demonstrations. In March 1965, during a fiercely opposed drive to register black voters, Martin Luther King Jr. led a protest march from Selma to the state capital, Montgomery, which was marked by brutal bludgeonings of civil rights demonstrators.

it was mighty discouraging.

The civil rights movement was a time when we thought: Maybe now it will finally happen. Maybe now our country will finally grow up, come to terms with this race mess. But it seems like the momentum was lost when the Vietnam War happened. It was like all the energy of the young people, and the focus of the country, got shifted away from civil rights.

Sadie and I were very upset by that whole Vietnam mess. We had a great-nephew in Vietnam who was not the same after he came home. His life just went down the drain. Vietnam just seemed like one big mistake. Politicians are not like normal people. They don't say, "Sorry, I made a mistake." They don't know how to admit when they're wrong, and fix the situation.

But it wasn't just Vietnam that slowed down the progress we made in the civil rights movement, in my opinion. It had a lot to do with lack of leadership after Martin Luther King died. Things have kind of slid downhill as far as equality is concerned. The 1980s were the worst, yes, sir!

Sadie and I are registered Independents, and we usually favor the Democrats, like Mr. Clinton. We loved Jimmy Carter because he was an honest man, and his heart was in the right place. Another president we liked was Lyndon Johnson, because we believe he sincerely tried to help our people with his War on Poverty. And I liked Harry Truman; I surely liked that "Buck Stops Here" business.

I'll tell you something, honey: I would have

made a very good president. That's right! *Me!* I would have done well. I'm honest and I'm tough and I could get the job done, yes, sir!

The first thing I would do if I was president would be to say that people over one hundred years of age no longer have to pay taxes! Ha ha! Lord knows I've paid my share.

Seriously, the first thing I would do if I was president would be to get rid of this old deficit. That funny little white guy, Ross Perot, he is right about the deficit. We are a foolish, foolish people. That deficit is a disgrace. I heard on the radio that every two seconds, our debt increases a million dollars. When I heard that, it got me so upset I could not sleep that night. It just about worried me to death.

I guess it will be a thousand years — probably never — before a colored person is elected president of the United States. Sadie disagrees with me. She says, "There will be a Negro president someday."

That reminds me of a song that white minstrels in blackface would sing to make fun of Negroes, back in the 1890s:

Oh my, what fun
In Washington
I bettya every coon
From coontown will be there
Oh my, what fun
In Washington
When the coon sits in that presidential
    chair.

255

See, I think white people would rather die than vote for a Negro president. I predict there will be a white woman president before there is a Negro president. And if a Negro is elected president? That person will be a Negro *woman*.

How do I know this? I'm a little psychic. Like with that Clarence Thomas mess, the Supreme Court nomination. He's lying. That girl, Anita Hill, is telling the *truth*. And Sadie says, "How do you know?" Well, I'll tell you something: Honey, I know a rascal when I see one!

Sadie and I watched the whole thing on the TV, and when I saw all those silly old white men asking those stupid questions I almost got myself on a train and went down to Washington. I could have straightened out that whole Clarence Thomas mess in ten minutes, yes, sir! I should have gotten myself on a train and gone on down there, but Sadie wouldn't let me.

So you see that I still have the urge to change the world. The truth is, you're born a certain way and there's some things you can change, and some things you can't.

31

SADIE

One thing I've noticed since I got this old is that I have started to dream in color. I'll remember that someone was wearing a red dress or a pink sweater, something like that. I also dream more than I used to, and when I wake up I feel tired. I'll say to Bessie, "I sure am tired this morning. I was teaching all night in my dreams!"

Bessie was always the big dreamer. She was always talking about what she dreamed the night before. She has this same dream over and over again, about a party she went to on Cotton Street in Raleigh, way back when. Nothing special happens; she just keeps dreaming she's there. In our dreams, we are always young.

Truth is, we both forget we're old. This happens all the time. I'll reach for something real quick, just like a young person. And realize my reflexes are not what they once were. It surprises me, but I can't complain. I still do what I want, pretty much.

These days, I am usually the first one awake

in the morning. I wake up at six-thirty. And the first thing I do when I open my eyes is smile, and then I say, "Thank you, Lord, for another day!"

If I don't hear Bessie get up, I'll go into her room and wake her. Sometimes I have to knock on her headboard. And she opens her eyes and says, "Oh, Lord, another day?!" I don't think Bessie would get up at all sometimes, if it weren't for me. She stays up late in her room and listens to these talk-radio shows, and she doesn't get enough sleep.

In the mornings, Monday through Friday, we do our yoga exercises. I started doing yoga exercises with Mama about forty years ago. Mama was starting to shrink up and get bent down, and I started exercising with her to straighten her up again. Only I didn't know at that time that what we were actually doing was "yoga." We just thought we were exercising.

I kept doing my yoga exercises, even after Mama died. Well, when Bessie turned eighty she decided that I looked better than her. So she decided she would start doing yoga, too. So we've been doing our exercises together ever since. We follow a yoga exercise program on the TV. Sometimes, Bessie cheats. I'll be doing an exercise and look over at her, and she's just lying there! She's a naughty old gal.

Exercise is very important. A lot of older people don't exercise at all. Another thing that is terribly important is diet. I keep up with the latest news about nutrition. About thirty years ago, Bessie and I started eating much more healthy foods. We don't eat that fatty Southern food very often. When we do, we feel like we can't move!

We eat as many as seven different vegetables a day. Plus lots of fresh fruits. And we take vitamin supplements: Vitamin A, B complex, C, D, E, and minerals, too, like zinc. And Bessie takes tyrosine when she's a little blue.

Every morning, after we do our yoga, we each take a clove of garlic, chop it up, and swallow it whole. If you swallow it all at once, there is no odor. We also take a teaspoon of cod liver oil. Bessie thinks it's disgusting. But one day I said, "Now, dear little sister, if you want to keep up with me, you're going to have to start taking it, every day, and stop complainin'." And she's been good ever since.

As soon as we moved to our house in 1957, we began boiling the tap water we use for our drinking water. Folks keep telling us that it's not necessary, that the City of Mount Vernon purifies the water. But it's a habit and at our age, child, we're not about to change our routine.

These days, I do most of the cooking, and Bessie does the serving. We eat our big meal of the day at noon. In the evening, we usually have a milk shake for dinner, and then we go upstairs and watch "MacNeil Lehrer" on the TV.

After that, we say our prayers. We say prayers in the morning and before we go to bed. It takes a long time to pray for everyone, because it's a very big family — we have fifteen nieces and neph-ews still living, plus all their children and grand-children. We pray for each one, living and dead. The ones that Bessie doesn't approve of get extra prayers. Bessie can be very critical and she holds things against people forever. I always have to say to her, "Everybody has to be themselves, Bessie. Live and let live."

Bessie can be very kind, though she usually saves her kind side for children and animals. She has a little dog who belonged to someone in the neigh-borhood who didn't want him anymore. He's part Chihuahua and I don't know what else, and he has some nasty habits, but Bessie loves him. She never eats a meal without saving the best piece for her little dog.

I'll tell you a story: Not long ago the Episcopal bishop of New York had a dinner to honor me and Bessie. A couple of days beforehand, Bessie announced that she was going to bring a doggie bag to the dinner. I said, "Whaaaat? Why, Bess, people will think you're a peculiar old woman." And she said, "So what, maybe I am a peculiar old woman. I hear they're having prime rib, and I would die of guilt if I had prime rib and didn't save any for my little dog."

Sure enough, when they served the dinner, Bes-sie took a bag out of her pocketbook and started to cut off the nicest part of the meat. And the bishop, who was sitting right there, asked her what she was doing. Next thing I knew, the bishop was cutting off a piece of *his* prime rib and wrapping it in a napkin for Bessie's little dog, and everybody else started doing the same thing, because the bishop did.

When we got home, Bessie was so excited she was almost giddy. She kept saying, "I've got enough prime rib to feed my little dog for a week!" I said, "Well, I certainly hope he enjoys the bishop's dinner."

Before Bessie got her little dog, we had a stray cat we named Mr. Delany, since we don't have a man in the house. He had been run over by a car, and had crawled up on our doorstep. So we brought the kitty in the house, rubbed salve into his cuts, and splinted him up. We fed him by hand and fussed over him, day and night, for two weeks. And you know what? He was just fine. But one day, he ran off. Bessie's still grieving for that old cat. She says, "I know he must be dead, or he would have come back."

If only I could get Bessie to be as sweet to people as she is to her animals. Bessie can be a little bit nasty sometimes, you know. She thinks it's her God-given duty to tell people the truth. I say to her, "Bessie, don't you realize people don't want to hear the truth?"

One time, there was a woman in our neighborhood who was furious at her granddaughter for moving in with a boyfriend. This woman was running around the neighborhood complaining to anyone who would listen. I was sort of sympathetic but Bessie said to her, "You shouldn't be running all around bad-mouthing your own kin." Of course,

Bessie was right. But that poor lady was embarrassed and has avoided us ever since.

Another time, a priest was over here visiting us and I noticed he'd put on a little weight. I thought to myself, Uh-oh, I bet she says something to him. Well, when he was leaving, Bessie said, "Now, Father, it seems to me you are getting fat. You've got to lose some weight!" He laughed and said, yes, he knew he needed to go on a diet. When he left I said to Bessie, "What did you have to go and say that for?" And she said, "I care about people's health, and sometimes people need somebody to give it to 'em straight."

Bessie does not mince words, and when she has a strong opinion — especially when it involves me — she's not shy! Not long ago, one of our nieces died, and somebody was over here describing the place where she died. It was called a hospice, and it sounded awfully nice. I said, "Well, maybe when my time comes, y'all should take me to a hospice." But Bessie got real mad. She said, "You ain't dying in no hospice. You ain't dying nowhere but upstairs in yo' bed!"

Over the years, we've buried a lot of people. Even the generation younger than us is starting to die off. I don't know why I'm still here and they're not, but I don't fret over it. It's in God's hands.

You know, when you are this old, you don't know if you're going to wake up in the morning. But I don't worry about dying, and neither does Bessie. We are at peace. You do kind of wonder, when's it going to happen? That's why you learn to love each and every day, child.

Truth is, I've gotten so old I'm starting to get a little *bold*. Not long ago, some young men started hanging out in front of our house. They were part of a gang from the Bronx, and they just thought our dead-end street here was a good spot to play basketball and do drugs and I don't know what-all.

Well, Bessie said to me, "I'll go out there and get rid of them." And I said, "No, Bess. For once, I'm going to handle it. You stay in the house."

I went out the backdoor and around to the sidewalk where they were hanging out. And I said, "You boys better get out of here."

They were kind of surprised. And then one of them said, "You can't make us leave. This is a public street."

And I said, "Yes, it's a public street, but it's not a *park,* so get moving."

And this fella said to me: "Just how do you think you're going to make us go?"

I pointed to my house. I said, "My sister is inside and she has her hand on the phone to call the police." Of course, this was a little white lie because we don't have a phone, but they didn't know that.

So the leader of this group laughed at me and he said, "You think the police are gonna come when some old *nigger woman* calls them?"

I said, "Yes, they will come. Because I own this property here, and I own this house, and I pay my taxes. They *will* come, and they will boot

263

you on out of here."

Well, they grumbled and complained, and finally they left. They came back about a week later, and our neighbor ran them off. And they never did come back.

Bessie was kind of surprised that I took those boys on like that. To tell you the truth, so was I.

32

SADIE

I was mighty proud of Sadie for taking on those no-good fellas and running them on out of there. It just goes to show she can be tough when she puts her mind to it. I said to her, "Sadie, our Grandpa Miliam surely would have been proud."

I was just thinking about Mr. Miliam this morning. There was a cute little squirrel in my yard, and I said, "Oh, you better be glad Mr. Miliam and his gun ain't around. Cause he'd shoot you and fry you up for his breakfast."

You know how when you come up on a squirrel, it'll run around to the other side of the tree? Well, Mr. Miliam would send one of us grandchildren to chase the squirrel back around to his side, and he would shoot it dead while the child stayed hid behind the tree. But don't worry. Mr. Miliam was an excellent shot, and nobody ever got hurt.

I wonder what Mr. Miliam would think of his granddaughters living this long. Why, I suppose he'd get a kick out of it. I know he'd have lived longer if Grandma hadn't died and it broke his heart. Sometimes, you need a reason to keep living.

Tell you the truth, I wouldn't be here without sister Sadie. We are companions. But I'll tell you something else: Sadie has taken on this business of getting old like it's a big *project*. She has it all figured out, about diet and exercise. Sometimes, I just don't want to do it, but she is my big sister and I really don't want to disappoint her. Funny thing about Sadie is she rarely gets — what's the word? — depressed. She is an easygoing type of gal.

Now, honey, I get the blues sometimes. It's a shock to me, to be this old. Sometimes, when I realize I am 101 years old, it hits me right between the eyes. I say, "Oh Lord, how did this happen?" Turning one hundred was the worst birthday of my life. I wouldn't wish it on my worst enemy. Turning 101 was not so bad. Once you're past that century mark, it's just not as shocking.

There's a few things I have had to give up. I gave up driving a while back. I guess I was in my late eighties. That was terrible. Another thing I gave up on was cutting back my trees so we have a view of the New York City skyline to the south. Until I was ninety-eight years old, I would climb up on the ladder and saw those tree branches off so we had a view. I could do it perfectly well; why pay somebody to do it? Then Sadie talked some sense into me, and I gave up doing it.

Some days I feel as old as Moses and other days I feel like a young girl. I tell you what: I have only a little bit of arthritis in my pinky finger, and my eyes aren't bad, so I know I could still be practicing dentistry. Yes, I am sure I could still do it.

But it's hard being old, because you can't always do everything you want, exactly as *you* want it done. When you get as old as we are, you have to struggle to hang onto your freedom, your independence. We have a lot of family and friends keeping an eye on us, but we try not to be dependent on any one person. We try to pay people, even relatives, for whatever they buy for us, and for gasoline for their car, things like that, so that we do not feel beholden to them.

Longevity runs in the family. I'm sure that's part of why we're still here. As a matter of fact, until recently there were still five of us, of the original ten children. Then, Hubert went to Glory on December 28, 1990, and Hap, a few weeks later, in February 1991. That leaves me, Sadie, and Laura, our baby sister who moved to California with her husband.

Now, when Hubert died, that really hurt. He was just shy of ninety years old. It never made a bit of difference to me that Hubert became an assistant United States attorney, a judge, and all that. He was still my little brother.

Same way with Hap. You know what? Even when he was ninety-five years old, Sadie and I still spoiled him. When he didn't like what they were cooking for dinner at his house, he would get up and leave the table and come over here and we'd fix him what he liked to eat.

Good ol' Hap knew he was going to Glory and he was content. He said, "I've had a good life. I've done everything I wanted to do, I think I've done right by people." We Delanys can usually say that, when our time comes.

You know what I've been thinking lately? All those people who were mean to me in my life — all those *rebby boys* — they have turned to dust, and this old gal is still here, along with sister Sadie.

We've outlived those old rebby boys!

That's one way to beat them!

That's justice!

They're turning in their graves, while Sadie and me are getting the last word, in this book. And honey, I surely do love getting the last word. I'm having my say, giving my opinion. Lord, ain't it good to be an *American*.

Truth is, I never thought I'd see the day when people would be interested in hearing what two old Negro women have to say. Life still surprises me. So maybe the last laugh's on *me*.

I'll tell you a little secret: I'm starting to get optimistic. I'm thinking: *Maybe I'll get into Heaven after all*. Why, I've helped a lot of folks — even some white folks! I surely do have some redeeming qualities that must count for something. So I just might do it: I just might get into Heaven. I may have to hang on to Sadie's heels, but I'll get there.

The employees of G.K. HALL hope you have enjoyed this Large Print book. All our Large Print titles are designed for easy reading, and all our books are made to last. Other G.K. Hall Large Print books are available at your library, through selected bookstores, or directly from us. For more information about current and up-coming titles, please call or mail your name and address to:

G.K. HALL
PO Box 159
Thorndike, Maine 04986
800/223-6121
207/948-2962